Behavioral Sciences

(Sociology and Psychology)

for GNM Nursing Students

As per the New Syllabus of INC

Behavioral Sciences

(Sociology and Psychology)

for GNM Nursing Students

As per the New Syllabus of INC

Second Edition

Muthuvenkatachalam Srinivasan
PhD (INC Consortium), MSc Nursing (AIIMS, New Delhi),
D Pharm, RN (NMBA, Australia)
Associate Professor
College of Nursing
All India Institute of Medical Sciences (AIIMS)
Mangalagiri, Andhra Pradesh

Jyoti MSc (OBG)
Nursing Officer
Lady Hardinge Medical College and
Smt Sucheta Kriplani Hospital
New Delhi

CBSPD
Dedicated to Education

CBS Publishers & Distributors Pvt Ltd

• New Delhi • Bengaluru • Chennai • Kochi • Kolkata • Lucknow • Mumbai
• Hyderabad • Jharkhand • Nagpur • Patna • Pune • Uttarakhand
• Gujarat • Chhattisgarh • Punjab • J&K

ISBN: 978-93-94525-46-7

Reprint: 2027, 2026

Second Edition: 2025

First Edition: 2021

Published by **Satish Kumar Jain** and produced by **Varun Jain** for

CBS Publishers & Distributors Pvt Ltd

4819/XI Prahlad Street, 24 Ansari Road, Daryaganj, New Delhi 110 002, India.

Ph: +91-11-23289259, 23266861, 23266867 Website: www.cbspd.com

Fax: 011-23243014

e-mail: delhi@cbspd.com; cbspubs@airtelmail.in.

Corporate Office: 204 FIE, Industrial Area, Patparganj, Delhi 110 092

Ph: +91-11-4934 4934 Fax: 4934 4935

e-mail: feedback@cbspd.com

Branches

- **Bengaluru:** Seema House 2975, 17th Cross, K.R. Road, Banashankari 2nd Stage, Bengaluru 560 070, Karnataka
  Ph: +91-80-26771678/79 Fax: +91-80-26771680 e-mail: bangalore@cbspd.com
- **Chennai:** 7, Subbaraya Street, Shenoy Nagar, Chennai 600 030, Tamil Nadu
  Ph: +91-44-26680620, 26681266 Fax: +91-44-42032115 e-mail: chennai@cbspd.com
- **Kochi:** 68/1534, 35, 36-Power House Road, Opp. KSEB, Cochin-682018, Kochi, Kerala
  Ph: +91-484-4059061-65 Fax: +91-484-4059065 e-mail: kochi@cbspd.com
- **Kolkata:** Hind Ceramics Compound, 1st Floor, 147, Nilganj Road, Belghoria, Kolkata-700056, West Bengal
  Ph: +91-033-2563-3055/56 e-mail: kolkata@cbspd.com
- **Lucknow:** Basement, Khushnuma Complex, 7-Meerabai Marg (Behind Jawahar Bhawan), Lucknow-226001, Uttar Pradesh
  Ph: +0522-4000032 e-mail: tiwari.lucknow@cbspd.com
- **Mumbai:** PWD Shed, Gala No. 25/26, Ramchandra Bhatt Marg, Next to J.J. Hospital Gate No. 2, Opp. Union Bank of India, Noor Baug, Mumbai-400009, Maharashtra
  Ph: +91-22-66661880/89 Fax: +91-22-24902342 e-mail: mumbai@cbspd.com

Representatives

- **Hyderabad** +91-9885175004
- **Nagpur** +91-9421945513
- **Pune** +91-9623451994
- **Jharkhand** +91-9811541605
- **Patna** +91-9334159340
- **Uttarakhand** +91-9716462459

Printed at : Goyal Offset Works Pvt. Ltd. Haryana

CBS Nursing Knowledge Tree

Extends its Tribute to

Florence Nightingale

For glorifying the role of women as nurses,
For holding the title of "The Lady with the Lamp,"
For working tirelessly for humanity–
Florence Nightingale will always be
remembered for her
selfless and memorable services to the
human race.

Florence Nightingale
(May 1820 – August 1910)

About the Authors

Muthuvenkatachalam Srinivasan, PhD (INC Consortium), MSc Nursing (AIIMS, New Delhi), D Pharm, RN (NMBA, Australia), is currently working as an Associate Professor in College of Nursing, All India Institute of Medical Sciences (AIIMS), Mangalagiri, Andhra Pradesh. He obtained Doctorate in Psychiatric Nursing from INC Consortium (in collaboration with RGUHS, Karnataka) in 2017. He is a Postgraduate in Psychiatric Nursing from AIIMS, New Delhi and has also completed Diploma in Pharmacy. He is also a Registered Nurse with Nurses and Midwifery Board of Australia. He has published numerous research papers in national and international journals of repute. He is Deputy Editor of Indian Journal of Psychiatric Nursing. He has contributed chapters in textbooks and training manuals of Govt. of India. He is an executive body member of Indian Society of Psychiatric Nurses (ISPN). He received 'Best Researcher Award' from ISPN in the year 2016. He has attended IRON Program for Registered Nurses in Australia, International conferences in USA and Canada with travel grant from ICMR and conference organization.

Jyoti, MSc (OBG), is currently working as Nursing Officer in Lady Hardinge Medical College and Smt Sucheta Kriplani Hospital (SSKH), New Delhi. She has completed her MSc in Obstetrics and Gynecology from Rajkumari Amrit Kaur College of Nursing, New Delhi. She is an active member of Society of Midwives in India (SOMI) and has also worked as a stall demonstrator in National SOMI conference. She has made active presence in many conferences and has presented papers in several National conferences. She has contributed in various titles also.

Preface to the Second Edition

It gives us immense pleasure to present the thoroughly revised and updated Second Edition of **Behavioral Sciences for GNM Nursing Students (Sociology and Psychology)**. This edition reflects the latest advancements in the fields of Sociology and Psychology, aligning closely with the revised syllabus for the General Nursing and Midwifery (GNM) course as prescribed by the Indian Nursing Council (INC).

The study of Sociology and Psychology is indispensable for nurses, as these disciplines provide profound insights into human emotions, relationships, behaviors, and social structures. A comprehensive understanding of these subjects empowers nurses to connect with their patients more effectively, fostering better care and communication. As aptly stated by Thouless, "Psychology is the positive science of human experience and behavior." While Sociology delves into societal dynamics, psychology focuses on individual behavior, making their interplay highly relevant for nursing practice.

This book has been designed with utmost care to address the curriculum requirements and to present the foundational concepts of both Sociology and Psychology in a clear and precise manner. Written in simple and engaging language, the text ensures ease of understanding and practical application for GNM students.

Special emphasis has been placed on incorporating nursing implications, making the content directly relevant to the day-to-day responsibilities of a nurse. The material is structured systematically, supported by bullet points, flow diagrams, and relevant figures to enhance clarity and retention.

We have made sincere efforts to craft a comprehensive and student-friendly resource that meets the evolving needs of nursing education. It is our hope that this book will not only serve as an academic guide but also inspire students to apply their knowledge in meaningful and compassionate ways in their professional practice.

We are confident that this new edition will enrich your learning journey, and we look forward to your feedback and suggestions to further refine our efforts.

Muthuvenkatachalam Srinivasan
Jyoti

Preface to the First Edition

Sociology and psychology both involve the scientific study of people. Both fields provide insight into inherent human attributes such as emotions, relationships and behaviors. A nurse has to work with patients so she must be familiar with these inherent human attributes.

Knowledge of both the subjects, Sociology and Psychology, helps to get accustomed with patient's social relationships. In the words of Thouless, "Psychology is the positive science of human experience and behavior". Sociology studies society whereas psychology is concerned with human behavior, there are interconnections between sociology and psychology. Both are regarded as positive sciences.

The First Edition of "Behavioral Sciences for GNM Nursing Students (Sociology and Psychology)" is an effort to fill the gap in literature. The book is written in a precise manner.

This book covers the fundamentals of both the subjects with strict adherence to the revised syllabus for General Nursing and Midwifery course laid down by Indian Nursing Council. It has been expressed in a very simple language to make your reading an interesting experience. The content of this book is carefully planned and well presented with points, flow diagrams and relevant figures. Sincere efforts have been made to provide a comprehensive and structured content in this book within the boundary of present-day need. Nursing implications have been dealt in depth. We sincerely hope that you will enjoy reading this book as much as we have enjoyed writing it!

Muthuvenkatachalam Srinivasan

Jyoti

Acknowledgments

"Pleasure in the job puts perfection in the work."

—Aristotle

Started with writing a word and ended up writing a book, it was not a one day task rather it is a continuous effort of many helping hands throughout the way. That is how the art of writing with a blend of knowledge and immense support forms the strong base of this book.

Above all we would like to thank God for giving us this opportunity and capability for accomplishment of this book.

We would like to thank **Mr Satish Kumar Jain** (Chairman) and **Mr Varun Jain** (Managing Director), M/s CBS Publishers and Distributors Pvt Ltd for providing us the platform in bringing out the book.

We sincerely thank the entire CBS team for bringing out the book with utmost care and attractive presentation. We would like to thank Ms Nitasha Arora (Assistant General Manager – Publishing) and Dr Anju Dhir (Sr. Product Manager cum Commissioning Editor) for their publishing support. We would also like to extend our thanks to Ms Surbhi Gupta (Sr. Editor cum Team Lead), Mr Ashutosh Pathak (Assistant Production Manager cum TL) and all the production team members for devoting laborious hours in editing, designing and typesetting the book.

Editor and Contributors

Editor

Ratna Prakash (Chakraborty)
PhD, MSc (MSN), PGDHE, DRD
Dip. Med. Informatics
Professor & Academic Director
(Former Principal)
Pal College of Nursing and Medical Sciences
Haldwani, Uttarakhand

Contributors

Anju Dhir
PhD (Biotech), MSc (Micro), BSc (Med)
Ex-Lecturer (Microbiol)
Shivalik Institute of Nursing
Shimla, Himachal Pradesh
Sr. Product Manager cum Commissioning Editor
CBS Publishers & Distributors Pvt Ltd.
Delhi

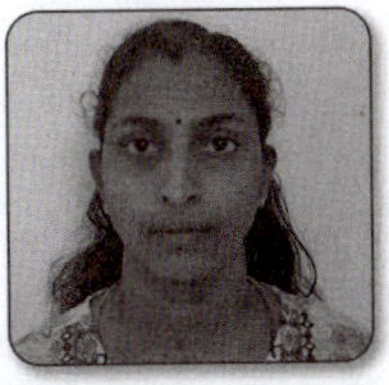

Anu C Vijay
MSc (Psychiatric Nursing)
Nursing Officer
AIIMS, Mangalagiri
Andhra Pradesh

Priyanka Malhotra
MSc (Mental Health Nursing)
Nursing Tutor
AIIMS Rishikesh
Uttarakhand

The names of the contributors are arranged in alphabetical order.

Special Features of the Book

LEARNING OBJECTIVES

After the completion of the chapter, the readers will be able to:
- Define sociology.
- Describe the scope of sociology.
- Understand the importance of sociology in nursing.
- Interpret the relationship between sociology and other sciences.

Learning Objectives given in the beginning of each chapter help readers understand the purpose of the chapter.

CHAPTER OUTLINE

- Scope of Sociology
- Special Branches of Sociology
- Relationship of Sociology with Other Social Sciences
- Uses of Sociology for Nurses

Chapter Outline gives a glimpse of the content covered in the chapter.

KEY TERMS

Anthropology: Anthropology is the scientific study of humans, their behavior, and societies in the past and present.

Economics: A social science concerned with the production, distribution, and consumption of goods and services.

Key Terms are added in each chapter to help understand the difficult scientific terms in easy language.

TABLE 5.1: Differences between the tribe and clans

Characteristics	Tribes	Clans
Geographical area	Tribes live in a definite geographical area	They do not have a definite geographical area
Language	Language is common	Language is not common

Numerous **Tables** have been used in the chapters to facilitate learning in a quick way.

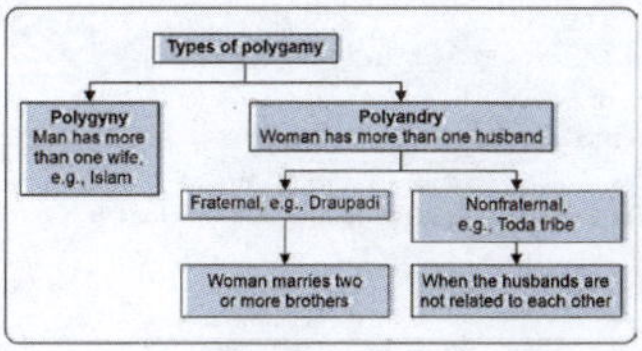

FIGURE 4.2: Types of polygamy

The book is well illustrated with relevant **Figures/ Flowcharts** for easy grasp of the relevant topic.

DEFINITIONS

- "Marriage is the approval of social pattern whereby two or more persons establish a family."
  —Horton and Hunt
- "Marriage is a stable relationship in which a man and a woman are socially permitted to have children."
  —Johnson

Important **Definitions** are incorporated to gain in-depth knowledge.

Do you know?

3 R's while forming a new habit and breaking bad habit

- **Reminder/Resolve:** Resolution is a strong decisive step that is taken for a purposeful action. Resolution depends on belief in the ability to complete tasks and reach goals.
- **Routine/Rehearse:** Rehearsing the new habit helps in the formation of habit.
- **Reward/Repeat:** A new behavior only becomes a habit once it has been repeated for enough times to make it an automatic behavior.

Do you know? boxes provide highly useful additional information to enhance the knowledge of the student.

SUMMARY

- Various sociological phenomena are studied under the umbrella of sociology.
- "Sociology is a special branch of knowledge dealing with the ultimate forms of mental or psychic relationships, which unite people in society."

Important takeaway points of respective chapters have been highlighted under **Summary** boxes.

STUDENT ASSIGNMENT

LONG ANSWER QUESTIONS

1. How is sociology useful for nurses?
2. Describe the sociology in relation to other sciences.

SHORT ANSWER QUESTIONS

1. Define sociology.
2. Describe the scope of sociology.

MULTIPLE CHOICE QUESTIONS

1. **Who coined the term "sociology" and is considered as the Father of Sociology?**
   a. Karl Marx   b. Auguste Comte
   c. Max Weber   d. Emile Durkheim
2. **Scope of sociology is studied as per the views of:**
   a. Formalistic school   b. Synthetic school
   c. Both a and b   d. None of these
3. **Which School of Thought opined that sociology is a general science?**
   a. Synthetic school   c. Vienna school
   b. Formalistic school   d. Scientific school

Detailed **Student Assignment** in the form of exercises in each and every chapter will facilitate structured learning and revision of the material provided in the respective chapters.

Syllabus

SOCIOLOGY

Placement: First Year **20 Marks**

Unit No.	Learning Objectives	Content	Hrs.	Teaching Learning Activities	Assessment Methods
I.	Describe the nature, scope & content of sociology and its importance in nursing.	**Introduction** • Definition and scope of sociology • Its relationship with other social sciences • Uses of sociology for nurses	2	Lecture cum discussions	• Short answer • Objective type
II.	Describe the influence of the environment on individual development and the rights and responsibilities of the individual in the society.	**Individual** • Review of human growth and development • The socialization process • Effect of environment on human growth and development • Rights and responsibilities of the individual in a democratic society	2	Lecture cum discussions	• Short answer • Objective type • Essay type
III.	Describe the concept of family as a social unit.	**Family** • Definition, characteristics and types of family • Family cycle and basic needs of family • Importance of interdependence of family members • Important functions of family and their problems • Types of marriage, medical and sociology aspects of marriage	4	Lecture cum discussions	• Short answer • Objective type • Essay type

Contd...

Unit No.	Learning Objectives	Content	Hrs.	Teaching Learning Activities	Assessment Methods
IV.	Describe the social groups, social change, control, stratification and social problems.	**Society** • Definition and meaning • Social groups—types, structure, intergroup relationship group cycle, group behavior and group morale • Social change—meaning, factors affecting and effect on society and institution leading to social problems • Social control • Social stratification • Social problems—prostitution, crime divorce, dowry system, juvenile delinquency, drug addiction alcoholism, handicapped, over population and slum • Social agencies and remedial measures	8	• Lecture cum discussions • Visits to social institutions	• Short answer • Objective type • Essay type
V.	Describe the culture and characteristics of community.	**Community** • Community ▪ Definition and types ▪ Rural and urban • Culture and characteristics	4	Lecture cum discussions	• Short answer • Objective type • Essay type

PSYCHOLOGY

40 Marks

Unit No.	Learning Objectives	Content	Hrs.	Teaching Learning Activities	Assessment Methods
I.	State the concept, scope and importance of psychology.	**Introduction** • Definition, nature and scope of psychology • Importance of psychology for nurses	2	Lecture cum discussion	• Short answer • Objective type
II.	Describe the structure of the mind.	**Structure of the Mind** • Conscious, preconscious • Id, ego and superego	2	Lecture cum discussion	• Short answer • Objective type
III.	• Illustrate the dynamics of human behavior. • Describe the concept of mental health.	**Psychology of Human Behavior** • Basic human needs, dynamics of behavior, motivation drives • Body mind relationship, mental health, characteristics of mentally healthy person, emotional control, psychological problems of patients and relatives • Stress and conflicts, natural sources and types of stress and conflicts, dealing with stress and conflict, frustration—sources and overcoming frustration • Mental mechanism, their uses and importance • Attitude—meaning, development changes in attitude, effects of attitudes on behavior, importance of positive attitude for the nurse • Habits—meaning and formation • Breaking of bad habits, importance of good habit formation for the nurse	12	• Lecture cum discussion • Role play	• Short answer • Objective type • Essay type

Contd...

Unit No.	Learning Objectives	Content	Hrs.	Teaching Learning Activities	Assessment Methods
IV.	Describe and apply the process of learning, thinking, reasoning, observation and perception.	**Learning** • Nature, types and laws of learning • Factors affecting learning, memory and forgetting **Thinking and Reasoning** Nature and types of thinking, reasoning, problem solving, importance of creative thinking for nurse **Observation and Perception** Attention, perception, laws of perception, factors affecting attention and perception, and errors in perception	13	• Lecture cum discussions • Role play	• Short answer • Objective type • Essay type
V.	Discuss the concept and development of personality.	**Personality** • Meaning, nature and development, types of personality • Assessment of personality importance of knowledge of personality for the nurse • Characteristics of various age groups—child adolescent, adult and aged • Will and character	6	• Lecture cum discussions • Role play • Psychometric assessment	• Short answer • Objective type • Essay type
VI.	Discuss the nature and measurement of intelligence.	**Intelligence** • Definition, meaning, individual differences in intelligence • Mental ability, nature of intelligence and development • Assessment of intelligence	5	• Lecture cum discussions • Demonstration • Role play • IQ testing	• Short answer • Objective type • Essay type

Contents

Section I SOCIOLOGY

1

Introduction to Sociology

LEARNING OBJECTIVES

After the completion of the chapter, the readers will be able to:

- Define sociology.
- Describe the scope of sociology.
- Understand the importance of sociology in nursing.
- Interpret the relationship between sociology and other sciences.

CHAPTER OUTLINE

- Scope of Sociology
- Special Branches of Sociology
- Relationship of Sociology with Other Social Sciences
- Uses of Sociology for Nurses

KEY TERMS

Anthropology: Anthropology is the scientific study of humans, their behavior, and societies in the past and present.

Economics: A social science concerned with the production, distribution, and consumption of goods and services.

Political sciences: Social study concerning the allocation and transfer of power in decision making, the roles and systems of governance including governments and international organizations, political behavior and public policies.

Sociology: The study of social life, social change, and the social causes and consequences of human behavior.

Man is a social animal. Both the nature and the necessity make the man live in a society. Sociology is the youngest of all social sciences. The word "sociology" was coined by Auguste Comte, a French Philosopher in 1839. He is considered as the "Father of Sociology". The word "sociology" is derived from the Latin word **societus** which means 'being friendly with others' and the Greek word **logos** which means 'study of', hence, sociology means the study of human relations in a group and their interactions with each other in the society. Various sociological phenomena are studied under the umbrella of sociology. The study of social relations is the main interest of sociology.

DEFINITIONS

- "Sociology is the science of society or of social phenomena." **—L F Ward**
- "Sociology is the study of human interaction and interrelation of their conditions and consequences." **—Ginsberg**
- "Sociology is a science of social institutions." **—Emile Durkheim**
- "Sociology is the study of social life." **—Ogburn and Nimkoff**
- "The subject matter of Sociology is the interaction of human minds." **—L T Hobhouse**
- "Sociology is the study of man and his human environment." **—H P Fairchild**
- "Sociology in broad sense may be said to be the study of interactions arising from the association of living beings." **—Gillin and Gillin**
- "Sociology deals with the behavior of man in group." **—Kimball Young**

Based on the above definitions we can conclude that:

- Sociology is a science of society.
- Sociology is a science of social relationships.
- Sociology is a science of social actions.
- Sociology is a science of social life.
- Sociology is a science of human behavior in group.

On a whole, the common idea deduced from the above discussion is that sociology is the branch of science that deals with the scientific study of the human interactions in society.

SCOPE OF SOCIOLOGY

There is not a single opinion about the scope of sociology. The overall objective of sociology is to systematically know about how individuals and groups create a social relationship and how do they maintain and change it.

Career Opportunities

The career opportunities of sociology are limitless discussed as follows:

- One can expect career at research institutions, law firms, public health, welfare organizations, private business, international agencies, medical firms, educational institutions, advertising firms, survey and poling organizations, journalism and many more.
- Students with a bachelor's degree in sociology often secure employment as social researchers, case workers, paralegals, public relations workers, administrators, community organizers, public policy researchers, and data analysts.
- There are two main schools of thoughts regarding scope of sociology that exists among sociologists. They are as follows:

Formalistic School

The scope of sociology has been discussed and viewed by Albion Small, Alfred Vierkandt, Max Weber and Leopold von Wiese. According to this school of thought, "sociology is pure and independent" and sociology deals with the problems which are not dealt by any other social sciences.

- **Albion Small:** "Sociology does not study all the activities of society. The scope of sociology is the study of the generic (general) forms of social relationships, behaviors, activities, etc."
- **Alfred Vierkandt:** "Sociology is a special branch of knowledge dealing with the ultimate forms of mental or psychic relationships, which unite people in society." He further maintains that "Similarly in dealing with culture, sociology should not concern itself with the actual contents of cultural evolution but it should confine itself to only the discovery of the fundamental forces of change and persistence."
- **Max Weber:** "Sociology aims to interpret and understand social behavior but it does not include all human relations because all of

them are not social." According to him, "Sociology is concerned with the analysis and classification of types of social relationships."

- **Leopold von Wiese:** "The scope of sociology is the study of forms of social relationships."

Synthetic School

According to this group, sociology is a general science. This school of thoughts wants sociology to be a synthesis (mixture) of the social sciences or a general science.

The other group states that the field of social investigation is too wide for any other social science and "Sociology is a special social science" such as Economics, Anthropology, History, and social psychology, etc. This also considers that "Sociology is a general science."

- **David Émile Durkheim:** Sociology can be divided into three major divisions:
  1. **Social morphology** that is concerned with geographical or territorial basis of the life such as its volume and density, local distribution and the life.
  2. **Social physiology** that is divided into a number of branches such as sociology of religion, morals, laws, economic life, language, etc. These activities are related to the various social groups.
  3. **General sociology** is concerned to discover the general characters of these social facts.
- **Sorokin:** "The subject matter of sociology is the study of relationship between different aspects of social phenomenon such as the study of understanding the relationship between the various social and nonsocial aspects."
- **J B McKee:** "Social action, social structure, social process and social institutions are included in the scope of sociology."

SPECIAL BRANCHES OF SOCIOLOGY

There are some special branches of sociology that are listed as follows:

- Medical sociology
- Social psychiatry
- Industrial sociology
- Political sociology
- Military sociology
- Economic sociology

RELATIONSHIP OF SOCIOLOGY WITH OTHER SOCIAL SCIENCES

Different social sciences deal with different aspects of man's social life such as history, anthropology, social psychology, economics, political sciences, etc., so these social sciences are closely inter-related. Sociology is neither a new science nor the mother of other social sciences but it runs parallel to mother sciences as discussed below.

Sociology and History

History is basically concerned with what happened in the past at a particular moment, and historian also wants to know how does it affected the future, though he/she is not interested to know future and present but how things evolved is definitely a matter of concern. History acts as a base of the present and as a predictor of the future.

Sociology is the science of the society and is interested in knowing how the society evolved and how the practices and cultures came into existence, and how does the various beliefs and practices affected the health of an individual, family and community.

Sociology and Political Science

These two are very closely related. Sociology has roots in politics. Sociology is a science of society but political science is the science of state and government.

- Sociology deals with all kinds of the societies both organized and unorganized, whereas political science deals only with the politically organized societies.
- Sociology has a wider scope than political science. Sociology studies man as a "social animal" whereas in political science man is considered as a political animal.
- Sociology is a general social science but political science is a special social science.
- The approach of sociology is sociological whereas the approach of political science is political.
- Sociology is comparatively younger science than political science.

Sociology and Anthropology

The sociology and anthropology are connected to each other. Anthropology is also defined as "the science of man and his works and behavior." It deals with men in groups not individuals. There are two types of anthropology:

1. **Organic or physical anthropology:** It deals with the evolution of the man, his bodily characteristics and heredity.
2. **Sociocultural anthropology:** It is often called cultural anthropology and it studies man as a social animal. Hobel says that "Sociology and anthropology are in their broadest sense one and the same. Origin of the family, beginning of the marriage, private property, etc., can be understood better in the light of anthropological knowledge. The conclusions drawn by the sociologists have helped anthropologists in their studies."
    - Sociologists study both small and large societies.
    - Anthropologists generally concentrate on small societies.

Sociology and Psychology

Sociology and psychology are interrelated sciences. Psychology is the study of human behavior. Some psychologists dispute the relationships between sociology and psychology.

- According to Durkheim, "Sociology deals with the social facts not with the psychological facts."
- Ginsberg's sociological explanations can be confirmed by relating them to the psychological laws as an explanation.
- According to Krech and Crutchfield, "Social psychology is the science of behavior of an individual in the society." Social psychology depends on sociology to understand properly human nature and behavior. At the same time, it has been widely recognized that for understanding the changes in social structure, psychological factors play important role. Both sciences have common topics. Social psychology also helps to face the social problems.
- Psychology is a behavioral science that generally deals with individuals. Social psychology serves as a link between sociology and psychology. Sociology studies the society and social groups. Social psychology studies the behavior of an individual.

Sociology analyzes social processes but social psychology analyzes mental processes. Sociology takes interest in the social forms and structures where behavior of man takes place. Psychology and social psychology refers to the behavior and individuals directly. Sociology studies the groups themselves whereas psychology studies the individual. The social psychology deals with the behavior of an individual in a group.

Sociology and Economics

The relationship between these two are so close that sometimes one is considered as a branch of the other. Economics deals with the economic activities of man. Economics studies man as a wealth getter and wealth disposer. Sociology and economics are mutually helpful. Economical changes have been explained by some economists as an aspect of the social change. Many economists like Karl Marx and Veblen said that social phenomenon is determined by the economic factors.

Sociology studies all types of social relations whereas economics deals with only those social issues which are economic in character. The scope of sociology is wider than the scope of economics. Sociology is one of the recently originated fields but economics has reached advanced degree of maturity.

USES OF SOCIOLOGY FOR NURSES

The uses of sociology are shown in Figure 1.1.

- Sociology is used by a nurse for the scientific study of society.
- Sociology is used to study the role of the institutions in the individual development.
- Sociology is inseparable for understanding and it is utilized for making plans for society and according to the needs of society.
- Sociology is used in framing and analyzing the various solutions of social problems.
- Sociology helps to draw nurse's attention to the human dignity and toward the basic human needs.
- Sociology has changed outlook with regard to the problems in society like crime, etc.

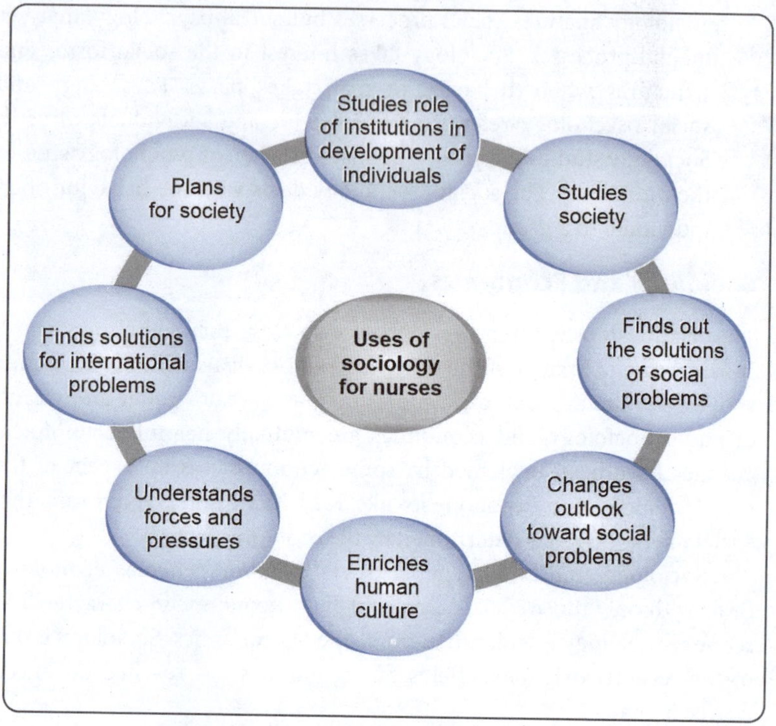

FIGURE 1.1: Uses of sociology for nurses

- Sociology has made significant contribution to enrich human culture and values. This developmental change further provides a way to understand existing problems in society.
- A nurse takes the help of sociology in the process of solving the global problems prevalent in different societies.
- The academic nature of sociology allows nurses to develop intellectual and critical thinking skills.
- Nurses must have an understanding of their client base if they are to deliver the best service. Sociology helps in this.
- Sociology is also included in the curriculum of nursing because health is integral social component. Most of the illness has social causes and social effects also. Sociology gives basic knowledge to deal with patient and to understand their habits, norms, culture and values, etc. It is important for a nurse to understand the importance of changing environment or surrounding.

- Sociology also helps the nurse to provide the need-based, individualistic care as listed in the nursing code of ethics also.

Hence, the knowledge of sociology helps nurse to avoid prejudices and discrimination. A nurse should understand the importance of social position, status and social responsibilities in health field by studying sociology. He/she has to work in accordance with rules and norms of society. The nurse should understand the necessity of changing environment to hasten the patient recovery. Social correlation of illness includes various demographic factors, which can be understood by the nurse with the knowledge of sociology. It helps the nurse to approach the patient at various domains such as:

- **Emotional domain:** The nurse should understand the patient's emotions as it helps in building a better interpersonal relationship and also helps to build the trust on a nurse. It helps the patient to vent out and participate in plan of care, which further alleviates the emotional burden and anxiety of patient.
- **Cultural domain:** It is difficult for the patient to adjust with hospital environment because of limitation of cultural environment.

  Example: A Muslim patient has to practice the *Namaz* which makes it difficult for him to practice in hospital. The nurse here can help the patient to practice the religious practices in the prayer room, etc.
- **Intellectual domain:** It is difficult for the patient to understand the nurse's and the doctor's point of view but the knowledge of sociology helps the nurse to understand the social background of patient and make him/her better understand the facts. The nurse can also modify the cultural practices to the therapeutic behavior, which further helps in the health attainment of individual and society.

SUMMARY

- Various sociological phenomena are studied under the umbrella of sociology.
- "Sociology is a special branch of knowledge dealing with the ultimate forms of mental or psychic relationships, which unite people in society."
- Sociology is a science of society but political science is the science of state and government.
- Sociology is inseparable for understanding and it is utilized for making plans for society and according to the needs of society.
- Nurses must have an understanding of their client base if they are to deliver the best service. Sociology helps in this.
- Social correlation of illness includes various demographic factors, which can be understood by the nurse with the knowledge of sociology.
- The nurse should understand the patient's emotions as it helps in building a better interpersonal relationship and also helps to build the trust on a nurse.
- The nurse can also modify the cultural practices to the therapeutic behavior, which further helps in the health attainment of individual and society.

STUDENT ASSIGNMENT

LONG ANSWER QUESTIONS

1. How is sociology useful for nurses?
2. Describe the sociology in relation to other sciences.

SHORT ANSWER QUESTIONS

1. Define sociology.
2. Describe the scope of sociology.

MULTIPLE CHOICE QUESTIONS

1. Who coined the term "sociology" and is considered as the Father of Sociology?

a. Karl Marx b. Auguste Comte
c. Max Weber d. Emile Durkheim

2. Scope of sociology is studied as per the views of:

a. Formalistic school b. Synthetic school
c. Both a and b d. None of these

3. Which School of Thought opined that sociology is a general science?

a. Synthetic school c. Vienna school
b. Formalistic school d. Scientific school

4. Who among the following prominent thinkers belongs to Synthetic School of Thought?

a. Bourdieu c. Sorokin
b. Comte d. Montesquieu

5. Albion W Small is a prominent sociologist in the first ....School of Thought?

a. Formalistic c. Vienna
b. Mercantilism d. Chicago

6. .... is an impersonal way of control.

a. Informal
b. Formal
c. Kinship
d. Family

7. .... is the family that extends beyond the nuclear family.

a. Extended family
b. Joint family
c. Nuclear family
d. Neo local family

ANSWER KEY

1. b **2.** c **3.** c **4.** c **5.** d **6.** b **7.** a

2

Individual

LEARNING OBJECTIVES

After the completion of the chapter, the readers will be able to:

- Review of human growth and development.
- Know about the socialization process.
- Describe the influence of environment on individual development.
- Enlist the rights and responsibilities of an individual in the society.
- Analyze the process of socialization and individualization.

CHAPTER OUTLINE

- Review of Human Growth and Development
- Effects of Social Environment on Human Growth and Development
- Socialization Process
- Rights and Responsibilities of an Individual in a Democratic Society
- Individualization

KEY TERMS

Development: A process that creates growth, progress, positive change or the addition of physical, economic, environmental, social and demographic components.

Growth: A stage or condition or process of increasing, developing or maturing.

Individual: A single human being as distinct from a group.

Individualization: To adapt to the needs or special circumstances of an individual.

Socialization: The activity of mixing socially with others.

An individual is a person with unique identity, may be similar to siblings but not exactly same except in case of twins. One individual is particularly different from other one and have his/her own needs or goals and likewise functions in society. Humans are social animals and cannot live in isolation. But being an individual, the structural and functional units of the society are studied, separately.

REVIEW OF HUMAN GROWTH AND DEVELOPMENT

Growth and development both are dynamic processes. They are often used interchangeably. These terms have different meanings. Growth and development are interdependent and interrelated processes. For example, growth generally takes place during the first 20 years of life whereas development continues after that too.

Growth

- It is a physical change and increase in size.
- It can be measured quantitatively.
- Indicators of growth include height, weight, bone size, and dentition.
- Growth rates vary during different stages of growth and development.
- The growth rate is rapid during the prenatal, neonatal, infancy and adolescent stages and slows during childhood.
- Physical growth is minimal during adulthood.

Rules of Growth

- Growth is a continuous and orderly process.
- Growth pattern of every individual is unique.
- Different body tissues grow at different rates.

Development

- It is an increase in the complexity of function and skill progression.
- It is the capacity and skill of a person to adapt according to the environment.
- Development is the behavioral aspect of growth.

Rules of Development

- Development is a continuous process.
- Development depends upon the maturation of nervous system.

- The sequence of attainment of milestone is same in all children.
- The process of development progresses in cephalocaudal manner.
- Development is proximodistal direction.
- Certain primitive reflexes have to be lost before attainment of relevant milestone.
- The initial disorganized mass activity is gradually replaced by specific and willful actions.

Stages of Growth and Development

Various stages of growth and development are (Fig. 2.1) as following:

- **Infant (infancy):** The period from one month after birth till one year of age is termed as infancy and the baby in this phase is termed as an infant. This is the period of rapid growth. When the baby is born, he/she is completely dependent on the mother and family members but as the child grows the dependency gradually decreases.

  The child starts recognizing the care provider and learns the basic social behavior in infancy. The milestones of development are usually classified into three categories: Motor development, language development, and social/emotional development.

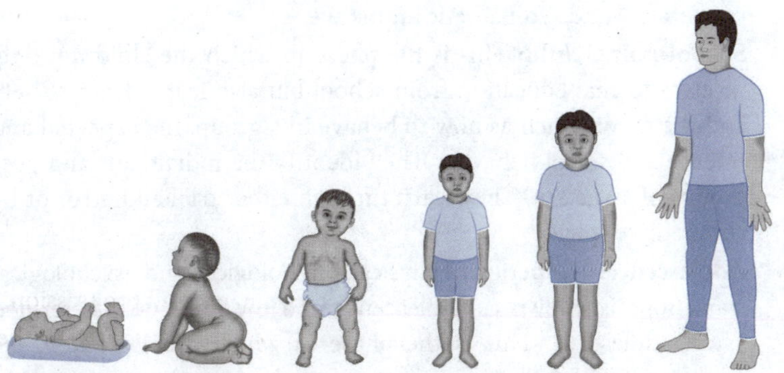

FIGURE 2.1: Stages of growth and development

Infant shows the emotions of jealousy, love and affection, stranger anxiety and anger. Some of the milestones of the infant are:

- The infant holds the neck (3–4 months)
- Sitting with support (5–6 months)
- Sitting without support (6–8 months)
- Stands with support (8–10 months)
- Stands without support and starts walking by the age of 12 months. The birth weight triples and length increases by 50% with respect to the birth weight and length respectively.

- **Toddler:** The child in the period from 1 to 3 years of age is called toddler. The growth is relatively slower in this period as compared to infancy. The most important event of this phase is toilet training-bowel and bladder training. This age is prone for accidents and the toddler needs independence also that further predisposes him for the injury. The restrictions and overprotection of toddler should be avoided, as it increases the dependency in later life and toddler may not like to be restricted.
- **Preschool child:** The child from 3 to 6 years of the age is called preschool child. Along with the increase in height and weight, the child's cognitive ability also increases and the child becomes more attentive. The informal teaching is initiated from home; therefore, the home is also termed as the first institution. The child is commonly cooperative and sympathetic at this age.
- **School-going child:** This is the phase in which the child not only receives formal education from school but also learns from society and the family, such as how to behave in a group, the expected and unexpected social behavior. They identify the individuals and peer groups of same sex. They learn through either trial and error or by competitive spirit.
- **Adolescence:** The period of physical, physiological, and psychological transitions is known as adolescence and the individual is termed as an adolescent. This is the phase in which a child enters the adulthood. The important events of adolescence is appearance of secondary sexual characteristics such as breast changes and initiation of menstruation (menarche) in females and masculine changes in males.

Adolescent feels like adults and tries to mimic the actions of adults in behavior and do not want others to consider him/her as child.

He/she feels free and wants to explore every single thing; therefore, he/she needs a good guidance. He/she prefers to take decisions by themselves and may not like the interference of parents in his/her life. On the other side, parents may have ambivalence and conduct related problems with the adolescents.

- **Young adult:** This is the phase of life of an individual in which he/she attains the physical and psychological maturity. Adult is full of energy, enthusiasm, innovations and ambitions in life. Adults establish new family relations such as marriage and form their own family and they are no more dependent on their parents and earn their bread and butter by themselves. The understanding problems with parents resolve. Marriage is a significant event in life of an adult.
- **Middle-aged adult:** Life again starts changing in terms of responsibilities of the family, certain psychological and physical changes are again evident such as decrease in basal metabolic rate and cognitive function. Individual plans for later adulthood such as retirement plan or investment plan.
- **Elderly or later adulthood:** Individual assumes the responsibilities such as head of the family. This phase starts with the retirement from the job, people experience certain changes in this age such as loss of memory, diminished vision and hearing, less interest, loss of self-confidence, considering oneself worthless and weak. There is increased risk of injuries and infections in this age. However, mental problems like dementia is also very common.

Psychosexual Stages of Development

- **Oral stage:**
  - It is a stage which begins from birth till child is of 1 year.
  - It needs to be fed as it is helpless and dependent on others for its very survival.
  - The aim of oral stage is to establish oral dependency.
- **Anal stage:**
  - During this stage the child learns that one cannot totally depend on the mother for everything.
  - The child realizes that there are some things that it must do by itself.
  - The child undergoes toilet training, acquires other skills.

- **Oedipal stage:**
  - In this stage the child becomes a member of the family as a whole. The child learns to identify itself with the social role ascribed to it on basis of its sex.
  - According to Freud, the boy develops the 'Oedipus Complex' and girl develops 'Electra Complex'.
- **Latency stage:** By the beginning of this stage, the child learns to be independent in the daily routine at home. He/she learns social norms.
- **Adolescence stage:**
  - This stage starts with the onset of puberty and continues through the teenage years.
  - This is a stage of transition from childhood to maturity during which new patterns of behavior are learnt to meet the increased demands of the peer group and of adult society.
  - Adolescents learn new roles, behavior pattern and internalize new social norms.
  - The process of socialization from oral stage to adolescence is known as primary socialization.

Factors Affecting Growth and Development

- **Prenatal factors:**
  - Genetic factor
  - Maternal factor (maternal nutrition, exposure to drugs and toxins, maternal disease and infection)
- **Neonatal risk factors:**
  - Intrauterine growth restriction
  - Prematurity
  - Perinatal asphyxia
- **Postnatal factors:**
  - Nutrition
  - Infectious disease
  - Environmental toxins
  - Acquired injury to brain
- **Psychosocial factors:**
  - Violence and abuse
  - Maternal deprivation

- **Protective factors:**
  - Breastfeeding
  - Maternal education.

EFFECTS OF SOCIAL ENVIRONMENT ON HUMAN GROWTH AND DEVELOPMENT

The process of human growth and development is a continuous process, which is affected by various factors. These factors affect the growth and development either directly or indirectly. Nowadays, the technology helps to predict the growth rate in utero and also predicts the expected height and weight of the child in later life. There are following factors which affect the human growth and development:

- **Race and ethnicity:** Racial factors such as height, weight, color, and other physical features also influence the growth and development of a human being. There is different pattern of body growth and development among various cultural groups. For example, a child of American white race will be white, his/her height, hair and eye color, and all facial structures are governed by the same race.
- **Genetics and heredity:** Heredity and genes certainly play an important role in the transmission of physical and social characteristics from parents to child as they form the genetic makeup. Different characteristics of growth and development like body structure, height, weight, color of hair and eyes are highly influenced by genes and heredity.
- **Sex:** Sex is a very important factor, which influences growth and development. There is huge difference in growth and development between girls and boys. Physical growth of girls in adolescence period is faster than boys. Overall, the body structure and growth of girls are different from boys, for example, boys have more muscular body than girls. The other secondary sexual characteristics such as voice quality and growth pattern also vary significantly among males and females.
- **Socioeconomic status:** Socioeconomic status also affects the growth and development. It has been seen that the children from different socioeconomic levels vary in average body size at all ages. The families with high socioeconomic status provide better food, sanitation and environment to the growing child.

- **Family size:** It also influences growth rate as in big families with limited income and scarcity of resources sometimes because of which the children do not get proper nutrition and which in turn affects the growth and development of the child.
- **Nutrition:** Growth is directly related to nutrition. The human body requires an adequate supply of calories for its normal growth and this need of requirements vary with the different phases of development. As per studies, malnutrition is referred as a large-scale problem in India. They are more likely to be malnourished, hence, stunted growth is there. If the children are malnourished, this slows their growth process.
- **Hormones:** A large number of glands are present inside the human body. These glands secrete one or more hormones directly or indirectly into the bloodstream. These hormones are chemicals that are capable of increasing or decreasing the metabolic rate of the body. Hormones are considered to be a growth supporting substance and any disorder of glands or hormones-either from birth or acquired may affect the growth and development in two ways either it can lead to exaggerated growth like—gigantism or stunted growth like dwarfism. Major role is played by the growth hormone and the thyroid hormones.
- **Environment:** Air quality, water, sanitation, housing, ventilation, food and pollution, etc., affects the health of an individual. For example, the increasing air pollution affects the health of every individual, and as a leading cause of asthma and obstructive respiratory disorders in children. Good environment promotes the growth and development.

SOCIALIZATION PROCESS

- Socialization is a lifelong process which starts at birth and continues till death. At each distinct phase in life, there are transitions to be made or crises to be overcome.
- It is the socialization process that helps an individual make these transitions and adapt to the changing environment.
- The process of socialization includes the elements and agencies of socialization.

- Social order is maintained mainly by the socialization. If the individual does not behave in accordance with the norms of the group, he/she disintegrates. The process of socialization starts long before the child is born. The social conditions prevailing at the time of birth lays down the kind of life he/she has to lead. The parents' courtship, the customs concerning the pregnancy and birth and the whole system of cultural practices in the family are important for the child's growth.
- Direct socialization begins after birth, the reflexes act as a barrier in the socialization process as they are innate and unavoidable.
- Sex instincts are the sources of the human endeavors which further explain the human behavior.
- Urge is a dynamic force behind behavior, it is the beginning of the social processes.
- Incentives help to determine the capacity of human beings as there is no limit to human capacity. It is determined by the need and the motivation, which comes from the incentives.
- **Imitation:** Learning by acting according to seen behavior.
- **Identification:** The identification of self and others is very important step in the process of socialization.
- Language is also one of the important factors of the process of the socialization.

A child is born with some innate physical and mental capacities. If the environment of the family and the mental or physical capacities are not that good, he/she may not be able to make best use of the environment, a good school, social equality, political freedom, i.e., a suitable environment is necessary to create proper environment for making the child grow in a better way. The problem of sex related issues during adolescence is one of the problems of parent–child relationship. Man lives in group and while doing so he has to follow the traditions, belief, ideology and moral values of the group. Group influences also determine the growth of human personality; hence the socialization is an important aspect in the development of the human personality.

There are three elements of socialization:

1. The **physical and psychological** heritage of the individual.
2. The **environment** in which he/she is born.
3. The **culture** in which an individual's rearing is done.

Features of Socialization

Socialization is the process of learning group norms, habits and ideals. The important factors in this process of learning are:

- **Imitation:** It is copying the acts of others. It could be conscious or unconscious, spontaneous or deliberate. It is an important factor in socialization. Through this, the child learns social behavior patterns. Children have great capacity to imitate and they often do it indiscriminately.
- **Suggestion:** Suggestion is a process of communication in which the suggested idea is accepted without logical grounds. A child lacks the ability to think and reason and hence, he is highly suggestible.
- **Identification:** In the very early stages, a child cannot make any distinction between himself and his environment. Most of his initial reactions are just natural and spontaneous. As he grows older, he learns to identify through which he satisfies his needs. For instance, the legs with which he plays, the mother who feeds him, the brothers or sisters, who play with him, are all identified. The areas of identification increase with the age.
- **Language:** Language is the medium of expression. In the beginning, the child utters meaningless sounds but gradually the skill of language is acquired. Thus, in the process of learning, language is important.

Phases of Socialization

There are four phases of socialization.

1. **Primary and secondary socialization:** Primary socialization takes place in infancy and childhood. This is the most crucial stage of socialization, as the basic behavior pattern is learnt by the child at this stage. The child internalizes many of the socially approved values, attitudes, beliefs and behavior patterns of his culture.
   The primary stage consists of three substages:
   i. **The oral stage:** The infant builds up definite expectations about feeding time and learns to signal his/her pressing needs for care.
   ii. **The anal stage:** Begins more or less after a year of infancy. The child at this stage is trained to take over some degree of care for himself/herself such as toilet training.

iii. **The oedipal stage:** Begins roughly from the 4th year and goes up to puberty. This is the period when child becomes a member of the family, as a whole, all the roles in the family prescribed according to sex are internalized by the child. The child identifies himself with the social roles.

Secondary socialization starts from the later stage of childhood and goes up to maturity. Socialization is a continuous process, which takes place throughout the life of an individual.

2. **Anticipatory socialization:** It is the kind of learning which describes a person's future roles. Anticipatory socialization occurs when people anticipate their own participation in a situation imagining how others would feel, think and behave. Anticipatory socialization makes the individual expect his/her own participation in a social situation by watching how others would behave in that situation.
3. **Developmental socialization:** As an individual grows, he changes and molds himself according to the standards and the needs of the society. He identifies himself with the society, values, norms, way of life, instincts, etc., and these traits continue to be imbibed in him.
4. **Resocialization:** Resocialization or socialization is a process by which one's sense of social values, beliefs, and norms are re-engineered. Resocialization is a kind of learning, which involves the learning of new ways of thinking. Feeling and behaving that are completely different from one's previous way of life. For example, resocialization occurs when one converts into a different religion or joins army or is put in a prison.

Agencies of Socialization

The process of socialization is operative throughout the life. It is a process that begins at birth and continues till the death of individual. It is a continuous process. As the socialization is an important matter for society, child's socialization should not be left to itself but should be controlled through institutional channels. It is socialization, which turns the child into a useful member of the society.

There are two sources of the socialization for child:

1. The one who has the authority over the child.
2. Those who are equal in authority to child.

The society takes no chances while protecting the most valued parts of its heritage. The child learns something from his/her equals. He acquires cooperative morality from them. Both the authoritarian and equalitarian relationships contribute to the socialization of the child. The common agencies for the socialization of the child are:

- Family
- School
- Friends or playmates
- Church/temple/mosque

Socialization = Authoritarian relationships + Equalitarian relationships

Factors Affecting Socialization

The process of socialization is affected by many factors, these can be individual, social, cultural and environmental factors. Some of these factors are described below:

- **Individual factors:** There can be numerous individual factors. One may not feel confident in social situations because of class, caste, physical appearance, educational status, perception toward society, and lingual abilities.
- **Social factors:** Apart from the individual factors, there could be certain social factors also, which inhibit the socialization process. There could be poor interaction in the society due to poor social environment, behavior in the society, family type (good socialization in joint families), participation in social gatherings, view toward social norms, etc.
- **Cultural factors:** These are the various traditional and customary practices pertaining to one's own culture. Culture plays an important role in determining the process of socialization. When the child grows and notices these cultural practices then he/she tries to find out the reason behind certain practices. Sometimes when certain practices are found to have no explanation or they are not useful, then those practices are discarded and the individual stops following them, that leads to the hindrance in the process of socialization.

RIGHTS AND RESPONSIBILITIES OF AN INDIVIDUAL IN A DEMOCRATIC SOCIETY

Rights

A right is a privilege or freedom that is protected. Rights are not usually provided automatically; they are usually fought for and claimed. Example: Every child has the right to learn. Rights are the freedoms which are important for personal growth as well as for the society. Fundamental rights are a charter of rights contained in the constitution of the India. Fundamental rights aimed at overturning the discrimination and inequalities of pre-independence social practices. Originally seven fundamental rights were provided in the Indian constitution.

1. Right to equality
2. Right to freedom
3. Right to property
4. Right to freedom of exploitation
5. Right to freedom of religion
6. Cultural and educational rights
7. Right to constitutional remedies

The right to property has been removed from the list of Fundamental Rights through 44th Amendment Act.

Some other rights are as following:

- Every individual aged 18 years and above has a right to vote.
- Every individual who is born in the country and aged above 25 years can be a candidate for the elections irrespective of the educational qualifications or his status in the society. Rich and poor are treated equally.
- Weaker sections of society have reservation of seats and so they also have a say in the governance of the country.
- Minorities are suitably represented.
- Anyone who has the majority support in the legislature can become chief minister or prime minister irrespective of his caste or social status.
- There is freedom of expression to the individual and anyone can criticize the government without fear.

- Individuals in a democracy have the freedom to excel in any field like music and other arts and sciences. He/she is free to participate in any cultural activity.
- Individuals can join army and contribute their services in the defense of the country.
- Individuals have the right to practice any religion and there is no state religion so far as India is concerned as India is a secular state. All religions are treated equally. There is religious freedom.

Responsibilities

A responsibility is a duty or obligation. It is something you should do to show that you respect your rights.

Example: Your right to an education comes with the responsibility to show up to school prepared and on time. When an individual demands certain things as his right, he has certain responsibilities also (being answerable) and he must discharge them conscientiously and become the honest citizen of the country.

- Every individual should participate in the elections either as a candidate or voter. He should vote the candidate who is not corrupt and who can discharge the duties efficiently and sincerely. Caste or religion should not be considered here.
- Women should take part in the democratic process in large numbers so that they have due representation in all public bodies so that they can express their grievances forcefully and achieve what they want.
- Weaker sections of society should feel that they are not in any way inferior to others and exercise their votes judiciously so that only those who are interested in their welfare would come in power. They should not be swayed by the empty slogans of any political party.
- Minorities should also feel themselves secure under the democratic rule. They should exercise their rights in a proper manner so that people who have a soft corner in the welfare of these sections of people, get selected.
- Any individual who becomes a member of any legislature, parliament or any other public institution should consider himself as a public servant and discharge his duties without fear or favor.
- Individuals should exercise their freedom of speech in such a way that no section of people is insulted and the country's defence is not affected. The freedom of expression should be utilized for the good of society and the country.

- The individuals working in any field of activity should aim at achieving the greatest efficiency in that field and make a name not only for themselves but also for the country.
- Those individuals who go to foreign countries should behave in such a way that they bring the good name of their country.
- Religious freedom does not mean freedom to hate other religions. They should not only practice their religion faithfully but also respect other religions also. They should not give room for communal disturbances.
- Well-built youth of this country should join the defence force in a large number and use their might in the protection of the bodies of their nation.

INDIVIDUALIZATION

Individualization is the process by which an individual is made independent in his group. It is simply the process of attaining to one's own self. Socialization brings a man into relation with others. Individualization makes him independent and self-determined.

The process of individualization is carried out by the individual himself and this is mainly a mental process, which is spread through the prevailing ideas- are the two misconceptions to be removed first. Just because a man attains his own self, it does not mean that individual becomes completely free from the group. The task of sociologist is not only to ascertain the ideas that prevail at a certain time but also to find out how these ideas came into existence.

Aspects of Individualization

- The first aspect of individualization lies in the process of becoming different from other people. Democratization, free competition and social mobility also encourage individualization.
- Individualization includes being aware of one's specific characters and rise of a new kind of evaluation. The individual may consider himself superior to others and evaluate himself in high terms. It may be feeling of self-glorification.
- The third aspect of individualization is the wishes that goes through objects. Social mobility may also bind the individual to specific wishes. Family conditions may also shape wishes of the individual. For example, the feeling of becoming lonely may lead an

individual to introspection and inwardness. Especially in big cities, the community does not have much influence on the individual so he develops a feeling of privacy and partial isolation. It leads to individualization.

Factors Affecting Individualization

(Health problems associated with improper socialization and individualization).

- **Gender roles:** There is no distinction in male's and female's roles as per the law but the society has selected different functions for male and female as per the convenience. When a child grows as adolescent, he/she realizes his/her own gender and the expected social roles. When the person is not convinced with these roles there is problem with the gender and that causes abnormal social behavior.
  Example: If a female is not satisfied with her gender she may cross dress (being female, dress like a male) and may face identity crisis at some point of time in her later life. The same could be with males also but it is more common with females.
- **Lifestyle:** The lifestyle helps to determine the health status of an individual, and the routine practices such as type of diet, rest and sleep habit, bowel and bladder pattern affect the health and is also responsible for certain lifestyle related diseases such as: insomnia, diabetes mellitus, cancer, etc.
- **Employment:** The nature of job also affects the health status of an individual and it is found that apart from the infections and nutritional deficiencies there are many occupational diseases also.
  Example: Byssinosis (brown lung disease in cotton factory workers), plumbism (lead poisoning), etc.
- **Social relationships:** Good social relations help to boost the psychological health of an individual whereas poor social relations can predispose an individual to stress and related disorders such as psychosis, neurosis and mood disorders.
- **Health belief:** The health beliefs of an individual are formed from childhood. Parallel to the personality development, the belief about health also develop simultaneously which are relatively permanent and directly responsible for the health-related behavior.

SUMMARY

- An individual is a person with unique identity, may be similar to siblings but not exactly same except in case of twins.
- Growth and development are interdependent and interrelated processes.
- Development is an increase in the complexity of function and skill progression.
- The process of development progresses in cephalocaudal manner.
- The milestones of development are usually classified into three categories: Motor development, language development, and social/ emotional development.
- The child in the period from 1 to 3 years of age is called toddler.
- The child is commonly cooperative and sympathetic at preschool age.
- School-going children learn through either trial and error or by competitive spirit.
- The period of physical, physiological, and psychological transitions is known as adolescence.
- Adults establish new family relations such as marriage and form their own family and they are no more dependent on their parents.
- Elderly stage starts with the retirement from the job, people experience certain changes in this age such as loss of memory, diminished vision and hearing, less interest, loss of self-confidence, considering oneself worthless and weak.
- The process of human growth and development is a continuous process, which is affected by various factors, such as race, socioeconomic status. religion, sex, nutrition, environment, etc.
- The process of socialization includes the elements and agencies of socialization.
- Socialization is the process of learning group norms, habits and ideals.
- It is socialization, which turns the child into a useful member of the society.
- The process of socialization is affected by many factors, these can be individual, social, cultural and environmental.
- Rights are not usually provided automatically; they are usually fought for and claimed.
- A responsibility is a duty or obligation.
- Individualization is the process by which an individual is made independent in his group.

STUDENT ASSIGNMENT

LONG ANSWER QUESTIONS

1. Describe the effects of environment on human growth and development.
2. Enlist the rights and responsibilities of an individual in society.
3. Describe the process of socialization.
4. Describe the process of individualization.
5. Explain the agencies of socialization.

SHORT ANSWER QUESTIONS

1. Describe individual.
2. How does socialization influence an individual's identity formation and sense of belongingness in different social groups?

MULTIPLE CHOICE QUESTIONS

1. The process of social interaction by which people acquire the knowledge, attitudes, values, and behaviors essential for significant participation in society is called:

a. Culture
b. Defining the situation
c. Social communication
d. Socialization

2. The process by which an individual is made independent in the group is called:

a. Individualization
b. Growth
c. Development
d. Communication

3. Which of the following is not a characteristic of social group?

a. Its members are conscious of shared membership.
b. Its members accept certain rights and obligations.
c. Its members are a casual collection of people.
d. Its members have a distinctive set of interpersonal relations.

4. The response of individuals to one another is:

a. Culture
b. Ethos
c. Social interaction
d. None of these

ANSWER KEY

1. d **2.** a **3.** c **4.** c

3

Family

LEARNING OBJECTIVES

After the completion of the chapter, the readers will be able to:

- Define family.
- Describe the characteristics of family.
- Discuss the roles and functions of family.
- Explain the types of family.
- Understand family cycle.

CHAPTER OUTLINE

- Meaning of Family
- Characteristics of a Family
- Types of Family
- Functions and Roles of a Family
- Characteristics of a Healthy Family
- Family Cycle
- Basic Needs of Family
- Major Problems Faced by the Family
- Importance of Interdependence of Family Members

KEY TERMS

Family: A group of people related either by consanguinity (by recognized birth) or affinity.

Family cycle: A series of stages through which a family may pass over time.

Family is the basic structural unit of the society. Family is the most stable among all associations and institutions of human society. It plays an important role in the development of personality of an individual and also in the process of socialization.

MEANING OF FAMILY

A family (from Latin: Word 'Familia') is a group of people affiliated either by consanguinity (by birth), affinity (by marriage or other relationships), or by coresidence or combination of these.

DEFINITIONS

- "Family is a group defined by a sex relationship sufficiently precise and ensuring to provide for the procreation and upbringing of children."
  —MacIver
- "Family is a group of persons united by ties of marriage, blood or adoption, constituting a single household, interacting and intercommunicating with each other in their respective social roles of husband and wife, mother and father, son and daughter, brother and sister, creating a common culture."
  —Burgess and Locke
- "Family is a miniature social organization, including at least two generations and is characteristically formed upon the blood bond."
  —Summer and Keller
- "Family is a group of persons whose relations to one another are based upon consanguinity and who are, therefore, kin to another."
  —Kingsley Davis
- "Family is the biological social unit composed of husband, wife and children." **—Elliott and Merrill**
- "Family is a more or less durable association of husband and wife with or without children, or of a man or woman alone with children."
  —Ogburn and Nimkoff
- "Family is a system of relationships existing between parents and children." **—Clare**

CHARACTERISTICS OF A FAMILY

On the basis of above discussion, characteristics of the family can be studied under two broad headings:

1. General Characteristics

- **The mating relationship:** It is between a man and woman, then only the family comes into existence.
- **Marriage:** Institutionalization of mating relationship is done through marriage. Each and every family follows some rules or procedures through which it establishes the marital relationship by which family is formed. The selection of mate can be either by the individual as per his/her choice or even parents may select the appropriate mate.
    - **Nomenclature system:** Family identifies itself by a name. It also has a system of name giving. The new member of the family takes the name of the family through which the individual identifies himself. Mainly, it may be through the male line or female line. In other words, the descent may be known through the name of father, mother or both. Accordingly, the descent is known as patrilineal, matrilineal or bilineal.
    - **Economic provisions:** Each and every family is expected to have an economic provision to meet different economic needs of its members. Mostly, it is the duty of the head of the family to carry on certain practices to earn money and thereby fulfill the economic needs of its members.
    - **A common habitation:** Each and every family needs a common household to live in. Without a house, family cannot fulfill its tasks like child rearing. There are different rules for the establishment of residence. After marriage, either wife lives in her husband's parental home or she may reside in her own parental home which is called patrilocal and matrilocal residence, respectively or both of them may establish a separate home, which is known as neolocal residence.

2. Distinctive Characteristics

Following are the distinctive characteristics of a family.

- **Universal:** Families are found in all societies. Primitive and the modern, rural or urban may be different forms of it.
- **Emotional basis:** The love, affection, sense of belonging, inmate relationship and concerns show the emotional basis of the family.
- **Formative influence:** The family molds the character and personality of an individual.

- **Family size:** Family is a small social unit. The size may vary depending upon the members of the family.
- **Family members:** The roles in the family are associated with the rights and position in the family.
- **Social regulation:** Family is very important agency of social control and the group of families form the society.
- **Name system:** Each family is recognized by some name, which is very specific from generation to generation. The name continues and the members are known by that particular name only.
- **Descent system:** Descent refers to the origin of a particular family. It may be real or imaginary. Generally, inheritance determines the descent.

Thus the family is a biological unit implying institutionalized relationship between husband and wife. It is a universal institution found in every age and in every society. It is the primary unit from which the community develops.

TYPES OF FAMILY

The family in India is based on patrilineal descent, that means the children are identified by name and allegiance with the father's family. Property is passed on from generation to generation within father's family. Family structure has changed dramatically over the past few years.

Nuclear or Single Unit Family

The nuclear family is the old type of family structure. This family type consists of two parents and their children. Children in nuclear families mostly have more opportunities due to the adequate financial status of two adults (Fig. 3.1).

Advantages of Nuclear Family

- **Personality development:** Nuclear family plays an important role in the personality development of an individual. Children in nuclear family are closely attached to parents and they can have open discussion about their problems, which enhances the personality development of the child.
- **Status of females:** The female child and woman, both relish better living conditions and care in nuclear families than living in a

FIGURE 3.1: Nuclear family

joint family. A woman not only gets adequate time to look after her children but also she can plan and manage her house according to her own idea. There is no resistance from other family members moreover, the husband can also pay attention to the wife and children in a nuclear family.

- **Family planning:** Family planning programs are more successful in nuclear families as compared to joint families. The parents in nuclear family have to plan and limit their family in order to attain good financial control for the upbringing of their children.
- **Economical advantage:** The children get the ancestral property directly from their parents. The property is not claimed by the cousins.
- **Family environment:** The environment of peace and harmony helps to lead a pleasant family life ahead. There is less misunderstanding among the family members.
- **Responsibilities of family members:** In nuclear family, there are more responsibilities on the family members and the parents are obliged to take the responsibility of the children by themselves.
- **Family conflicts:** There are least chances of conflicts in family due to less number of family members and the elders being husband and wife only. All members of nuclear family are emotionally secured.

Disadvantages of Nuclear Family

- **Economic drawback:** The family property is divided equally among the brothers and as each live separately, they are compelled to hire servants or other helps to look after their ancestral properties.

Because of less number of family members, the work in field area is performed by the workers that causes increase in expenditure.

- **Children security issue:** In nuclear family, generally both husband and wife are engaged in work outside the house, therefore children are either neglected or looked after by servants or are left in the crèche. Child may feel lonely or emotionally insecure. They develop anxiety and if the bread winner is sick, dies or is not able to earn, in such situation there is no one to support the family. Even in time of emergency like accident, pregnancy and childbirth, family members are overlooked.
- **Socialization decreases:** The family is free from the direct control of grandparents, thus the grand children tend to develop bad habits like, disorganized lifestyle, and may behave in an indisciplined manner. Children become less social as they do not get opportunity to mix up with the cousins and the other members of family. Sometimes children may feel devoid of the tender loving care of the grandparents.
- **Loneliness:** The pervasive feeling of loneliness is one of the major drawbacks in a nuclear family. There is no one to share the problems and conflicts of the family members.
- **Security problem:** If the woman in nuclear family is widow, old or divorced, she may feel insecure and neglected.

Joint Family or Extended Family

The extended family structure consists of two or more adults who are related, either by blood or by marriage, sharing a common home. This family includes many relatives living together and working toward common goals, for example: business or raising the children. The families include cousins, aunts, uncles and grandparents (Fig. 3.2).

Advantages of Joint Family

- **Stable and durable:** The joint families are relatively more stable than nuclear families.
- **Personality development:** There is gradual and spontaneous development of the personality of the child which even went unnoticed, therefore the anxiety and stress among adolescents is less prevalent in joint families.

FIGURE 3.2: Joint family

- **Discipline:** The joint families are based on the principle of fair economy. Elderly family members impose a kind of informal discipline on each and every family member in order to maintain peace and oneness in the family. It maintains discipline.
- **Socialization:** Children in a big joint family form groups according to their matching ages and they study together, play together, quarrel together and are even punished together. As a result, the feeling of companionship grows that is free from any discrimination of one being a real brother or a cousin.
- **Care of elderly people:** Proper care is taken of elderly, widowed, physically weak and disabled family members. Old and elderly people are respected and looked after properly in a joint family.
- **Family environment:** The joint families have an environment of affection and unity and it is the best pattern of living.
- **Division of labor:** In a joint family, there are specific responsibilities for each member of joint family. The head of family has fewer responsibilities to take care of his family and the work is divided among all family members.
- **Provides recreation:** The joint family is an ideal place for recreation not only for children but adults as well. The festivals and other rituals in a family are celebrated together. These serve as recreation activities.
- **Provides psychological satisfaction:** Joint family gives a sense of completion, belongingness, and mutual trust among family members that provide the psychological satisfaction to an individual.

- **Agency for social control:** The joint family has a good control over the family members which in turn helps to achieve a social control.

Disadvantages of Joint Family

- **Economic instability:** It is often seen that only some of the family members actually earn and the rest passively feed on their income. High earning members often insult the low earning members.
- **Exploitation:** Some crooked family members may plot to torture and exploit another innocent and submissive members of the family.
- **Distribution of capital:** The high earning members often want their children to study in expensive schools (and they may need permission of head of the family for the same) whereas they don't want to share the burden of the children of other family members.
- **Lack of privacy:** The married couple in the family has less time to spend with each other in joint family, and the privacy is also less among husband and wife as they may not talk freely to each other.
- **Decision making:** In joint families, most of the important decisions are taken by the head of the family. Since, all the individuals within the family do not get an opportunity to participate in major decisions of the family, they often feel neglected and have low self-esteem.

Childless Family

There are couples who either cannot or choose not to have children. Childless families consist of a husband and wife living with each other (Fig. 3.3).

FIGURE 3.3: Childless family

Step Family

Because of divorce two separate families can merge into one new unit. It consists of a new husband and wife and their children from previous marriages.

Grandparent Family

Many grandparents raise their grandchildren because of variety of reasons. One out of fourteen children is raised by his/her grandparents. The reason could be parents' death, addiction, abandonment or medically unfit parents.

Single Parent Family

The single parent family consists of one parent raising one or more children on his/her own. Mostly a single parent family is a mother with her children or father with his children.

FUNCTIONS AND ROLES OF A FAMILY

The basic function of the family is to ensure the continuation of society, both biologically through procreation, and socially through socialization. The other functions of the family are as following:

- **Protection:** In all societies, family offers some degree of physical, emotional, and economical protection to its members. In society any attack on a member is considered as attack on family.
- **Love and affection:** The family is an integral part of an individual's life, as the needs such as love, affection and belongingness are learnt not from the books but from the family as it is rightly said that family is the first school.
- **Reproduction:** Each and every society depends primarily on the family for production of children. To continue generations family is required.
- **Socialization:** It is the family on which every society depends for the development and socialization of children in to adults who can later function successfully in the society. The child learns the social norms by imitation.
- **Satisfaction of sexual needs:** This is basic physiological need and is essential requirement of a couple living in a family. Sex instinct is

one of the needs of humans. The satisfaction of this need requires that both male and female should live together as life partners. It is the family where the husband and wife can satisfy their sex instincts easily and comfortably. A family not only satisfies but also provides the appropriate mechanism through marriage to regulate sexual behavior of male and female.

- **Economic function:** The family is the basic economic unit in most primitive societies.

CHARACTERISTICS OF A HEALTHY FAMILY

Characteristics of healthy family relations are as follows:

- **Love:** A child learns love and affection from mother and father only, basically from a family and as the child grows up he/she also demonstrates a selfless love for each family member.
- **Trust:** Home is the first institution to learn the basics of human behavior although human behavior is a very complex system but the family makes it very simple for the child to learn the behavior, manners, etiquettes, etc., throughout the life which are later on reflected in the society.
- **Peace:** Peace is being free from conflict, which is not an easy task in a family. But more important is the way we proceed toward those conflicts and, how much we care more about conflicts or the integrity of family. Sometimes holding your tongue in a potentially volatile situation or trying to sacrifice your wants, softly giving your opinions, listening to other member with patience can help a lot to solve conflicts among family members.
- **Patience:** Majority of family problems, social issues are all because of the lack of patience. When we are patient with one another, we can tolerate pains or trials calmly without complaining. The harmony of the family and eventually society can be maintained with little patience.
- **Kindness:** It is something which is always there in humans as a basic element of humanity but once we learn to be cruel and enjoy cruelty that just vanishes off the kindness. When family members act in a friendly way, it encourages everyone to do the same behavior every time.

- **Gentleness:** Another word for gentleness is humility. The Bible teaches that pride comes before destruction, and before honor comes humility. When family members put other family members above themselves then honor comes to the entire family.
- **Self-control:** When individuals practice self-control, then acting on the points above mentioned is possible.
- **Discipline:** It is the practice to obey rules. The child learns it by imitation. In order to teach the discipline to child, the parents and other family members need to be disciplined first. When families are disciplined in their actions then all members follow them. Else discipline in India is taught by using punishment to correct disobedience. The religion is an important aspect of society to maintain appropriate human behavior and to reduce the various social problems.

The family environment helps the individual to become not only holistic well-being but also a responsible citizen of society.

FAMILY CYCLE

The family cycle (Fig. 3.4) includes the following:

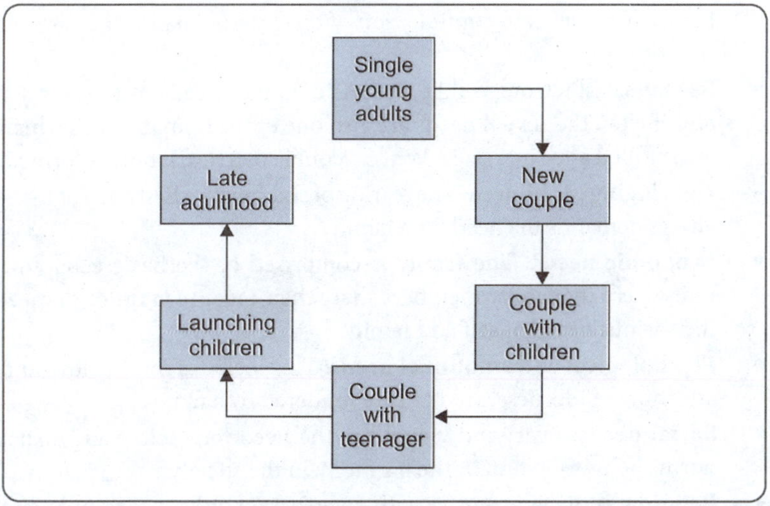

FIGURE 3.4: Family cycle

- **Single young adults:** The single and young adults are often considered as the basic units of family. These young adults attain the maturity in physical and physiological ways but the society has the norms to be single until marriage unites the individuals.
- **New couple:** When the young adults are united by marriage then they are regarded as a new couple.
- **Couple with children:** Once the couple has child and assumes a parental role *viz.* maternal and paternal roles, they work toward rearing of the child.
- **Couple with teenager:** The couple works toward the upbringing of the child. Slowly and gradually with time, the child grows as a teenager followed by the adulthood.
- **Launching children:** The parents help the children to work for the social identity and roles. Further the cycle of family continues as a separate unit after the marriage of the children, leaving the parents in their middle to later adulthood.
- **Late adulthood:** It begins after 65 years of age and beyond.

BASIC NEEDS OF FAMILY

- **Need for reproduction:** This need is felt in order to have one's own family. This helps in continuation of the paternal name and fame in the society.
- **Sexual satisfaction:** Unlike the basic human needs of food, water and shelter, the sexual needs are also one of the human needs which are fulfilled after marriage. When a couple marries, family is formed.
- **Upbringing of children:** The rearing of children in a best environment always demands the need for a family.
- **Economic needs:** The family is comprised of the basic economic unit where the family members share their income in order to meet the various needs of self and family.
- **Psychological and emotional needs:** This includes sharing love and affection, tenderness and the care rendered by a family.
- **Social needs:** Every individual has the need for society and social norms helps to maintain the harmony in the society.
- **Religion:** India is a country with diversity not only in geography but also in religion, languages and traditions also. As different religions have different needs and in order to meet those needs variety of religious practices are also there.

MAJOR PROBLEMS FACED BY THE FAMILY

Each and every family faces one or the other problem.

- **Abuse:** Abuse means not only physical injuries, but it also includes injury to the mind, and spirit. It violates the teachings of family and institution. Example: Elderly abuse.
- **Addiction:** The state of physical and psychological dependency is known as addiction, which not only affects the health of the person himself but also endangers other members of the family. Example: Alcoholism, smoking and drug addiction.
- **Suicide:** Due to poor coping skills and defense system the person in a family may not be able to cope up with the day to day stressors. Sometimes because of certain constraints, individual may not communicate his problems and take a drastic step like suicide.
- **Divorce:** It happens when the married couple cannot sort out the problems within themselves and declare their opposite counterparts as completely unacceptable. This situation leads to frequent conflicts in the relation, which ends marriage with mutual separation or divorce.
- **Lack of time:** Lack of time could be because of many reasons such as poor time management, race to earn more money, poor prioritizing and planning. The family members feel that they are either neglected or they are not significant. This provokes a sense of loneliness and pervasive sadness. Relations need time to nurture and if ignored can lead to family disputes.
- **Lack of discipline:** When the basic discipline and line of behavior is violated, it can cost irreparable damage in the families such as use of abusive language and lack of mutual respect.
- **Lack of communication:** Human being is a social animal and once he stops communicating his beliefs, feelings and opinions, it leads to a state of confusion and assumptions which are poisonous to the relationships. Therefore, communication is essential.
- **Financial burden:** Mostly head of the family feels that he is solely responsible for the finances of the family and if because of any underlying cause such as chronic or terminal disease, death or some other emergency one cannot meet the financial needs, it may lead to stress and anxiety. Example: It is common in case of huge business loss or lack of money as in case of crop loss or loss of limb in accident, etc.

- **Balance of work and family:** The balance between work and family is very important but at the same time it is not easy to maintain the balance.
- **Materialistic thinking:** In the present scenario, the human relations are kept at second place in life and the amenities are kept first. The modern human being craves to have luxuries and comfortable lifestyle, which leads to self-centered behavior. This thinking leads to dissatisfaction in life and the family and society are adversely affected due to this type of thinking.

IMPORTANCE OF INTERDEPENDENCE OF FAMILY MEMBERS

The members are the functional units of the family. Each and every family member directly or indirectly depends upon each other for fulfilling various needs such as love, care, belongingness, protection, culture, religion, and sexual needs of husband and wife- all are met within the family itself. Unlike the basic human needs, the family is equally important to meet all needs. The disintegration among family adversely affects the individual psychology to a great extent. Some of the offending behaviors may affect the integrity and harmony of the family, for example, smoking, alcoholism, domestic violence, abusive behavior, lack of mutual trust and respect may even become a cause for separation of family members.

SUMMARY

- Family is the most stable among all associations and institutions of human society.
- The family is a biological unit implying institutionalized relationship between husband and wife.
- The nuclear family is the old type of family structure.
- The extended family structure consists of two or more adults who are related, either by blood or by marriage, sharing a common home.
- Childless families consist of a husband and wife living with each other.
- Many grandparents raise their grandchildren because of variety of reasons.
- The single parent family consists of one parent raising one or more children on his/her own.
- The basic function of the family is to ensure the continuation of society, both biologically through procreation, and socially through socialization.
- The family environment helps the individual to become not only holistic well-being but also a responsible citizen of society.
- The disintegration among family adversely affects the individual psychology to a great extent.

STUDENT ASSIGNMENT

LONG ANSWER QUESTIONS

1. Describe the characteristics of the family.
2. Describe the roles and functions of the family.
3. Explain the types of family.
4. Explain family cycle.

SHORT ANSWER QUESTIONS

1. Define family.
2. What are the essential functions of family?
3. Define joint family.
4. What is extended family?

MULTIPLE CHOICE QUESTIONS

1. A group of people whose members are related by marriage, or adoption is a (an):

a. Family
b. Institution
c. Friends
d. None of these

2. Basic needs of the family include:

a. Need for reproduction
b. Economic needs
c. Psychological and emotional needs
d. All of the above

3. The system under which boys and girls are allowed to mix with each other and are given maximum permissible mixing facility by society before marriage is known as:

a. Probationary marriage
b. Experimental marriage
c. Compassionate marriage
d. None of the above

4. **If in a family, the offsprings inherit the mother's name, the family is called:**

   a. Matronymic b. Patronymic
   c. Matripotestal d. Matrilineal

5. **When the offsprings inherit the father's name, the family is called:**

   a. Patronymic b. Patrilineal
   c. Patriarchal d. Conjugal

6. **In .... family, the husband goes to live in the house of his wife.**

   a. Matrilineal b. Matriarchal
   c. Joint family d. Matripotestal

7. **Who among the following follow the matrilineal family system?**

   a. Nairs of Kerala b. Bhils
   c. Kadars d. Muslims

ANSWER KEY

1. a **2.** d **3.** a **4.** c **5.** a **6.** b **7.** a

4

Marriage

LEARNING OBJECTIVES

After the completion of the chapter, the readers will be able to:

- Define marriage.
- Describe the forms of marriage.
- Describe the roles and functions of marriage.
- Explain the medical and social aspects of marriage.

CHAPTER OUTLINE

- Forms of Marriage
- Functions of Marriage
- Medical and Sociological Aspects of Marriage
- Marriage in India

KEY TERMS

Marriage: A culturally recognized union between two persons, called spouses that establishes rights and obligations between them.
Monogamy: A form of dyadic relationship in which an individual has only one partner during their lifetime.
Polyandry: A form of polygamy in which a woman takes two or more husbands at the same time.
Polygamy: The practice of marrying multiple spouses.
Polygyny: The marriage of a man with several women.

Marriage, also called matrimony or wedlock, is a socially recognized union between spouses that establishes rights and obligations between them and their respective in-laws.

DEFINITIONS

- "Marriage is the approval of social pattern whereby two or more persons establish a family." **—Horton and Hunt**
- "Marriage is a stable relationship in which a man and a woman are socially permitted to have children." **—Johnson**
- "Marriage is relatively a permanent bond between permissible mates." **—Robert H Lowie**

Therefore, marriage is a socially approved institution which permits sexual relationships and procreation between a man and a woman.

FORMS OF MARRIAGE

Forms of Marriage on the Basis of Selection of Mate

- **Exogamy:** Society permits the selection of mate outside the clan, ***gotra*** and ***pravara***.
  A man should not marry a girl from the same gotra or pravara.
- **Endogamy:** Society puts restrictions on man to select a girl from his own caste or class.

Forms of Marriage on the Basis of Number of Partners in Marital Relationship (Fig. 4.1)

- **Monogamy:** A man or woman can have only one mate at a time. It is the most common type of marriage universally recognized.
- **Polygamy:** A man is permitted by the society to have more than one wife. It is due to some cultural pattern or socially accepted ways. In South India, in some communities a maternal uncle has right to marry his sister's daughter even though he already has a wife and children. When the first wife does not beget children, the man is permitted to marry another woman. In some cultures, because of higher economic status a man is permitted to have more than one wife.

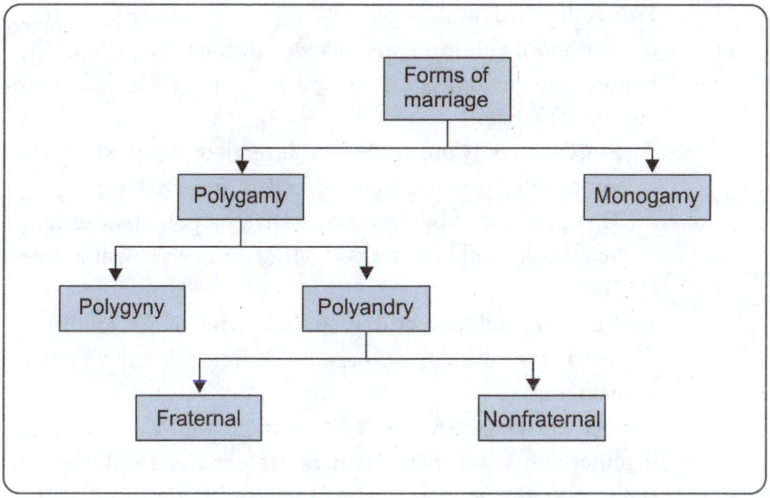

FIGURE 4.1: Forms of marriage on the basis of number of partners

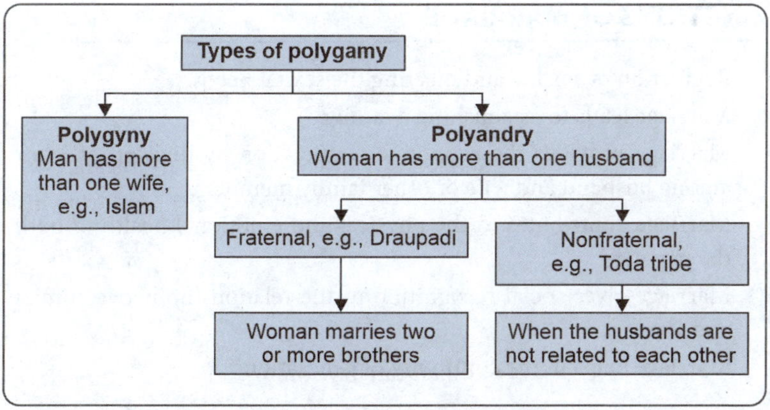

FIGURE 4.2: Types of polygamy

- **Types of polygamy:** The polygamy can be of following types (Fig. 4.2):
  - **Polygyny:** It is a form of marriage in which one man marries more than one woman at a given time. Polygyny is more common than polyandry.

- **Polyandry:** This system permits a woman to have more than one husband. This is mostly followed by the tribe people. This is prevalent in some northern parts of India due to certain cultural practices.
    - **Fraternal polyandry:** When several brothers share the same wife, practice can be called fraternal polyandry. This practice of being mate, actual, or potential, to one's husband's brother is called levirate. It is prevalent among Todas.
    - **Nonfraternal polyandry:** It is a type of polyandry in which several men who are not brothers, marry a single woman.
- **Group marriage:** A number of men and women come together and select their partners. Here men have the sexual rights over the women in the group and the viceversa. This type of marriage is found among Totem tribe of Australia.

FUNCTIONS OF MARRIAGE

- Regulation of sex life and meeting the sexual needs.
- Marriage leads to establishing a family.
- Marriage provides the economic cooperation by division of labor among husband and wife or other family members.
- Marriage contributes to the physical and emotional health of both the partners.
- Marriage gives social recognition to the relationship between man and woman.
- Marriage helps in the continuity of generations.

MEDICAL AND SOCIOLOGICAL ASPECTS OF MARRIAGE

Medical Aspects of Marriage

- Marriage, like other close relationships, exerts considerable influence on health.
- Marriage reduces the risk of cervical and breast cancer among females. This is strongly supported by the researches also.
- Marriage reduces the risk of depression among both men and women.

- Many researches have proved that married people experience lower morbidity and mortality across diverse health threats as cancer, heart attacks, and surgery.
- Research on marriage and health is part of the broader study of the benefits of social relationships.
- Social ties provide people with a sense of identity, purpose, belonging and support. Simply being married, along with the quality of one's marriage, are linked with mental health.
- The health-protective effect of marriage is stronger for men than women. Marital status—the simple fact of being married confers more health benefits to men than women.
- Women's health is more strongly impacted than men by marital conflict or satisfaction—unhappily married women do not enjoy better health relative to their single counterparts.

Sociological Aspects of Marriage

- The institution of marriage reliably creates the social, economic and effective conditions for effective parenting.
- Society permits the man and woman to live together and have child only after marriage.
- Marriage helps to maintain the synchrony and harmony in the family.
- Marriage is the turning point of the life for not only woman but for man too. As being married changes people's lifestyles and habits in ways that are personally and socially beneficial.
- Marriage is a "seedbed" of prosaic behavior (real behavior).
- Marriage helps in continuity of the generations in the society.
- Marriage gatherings help to unite people by certain practices such as rituals before and after marriage. All the relatives and the neighbors participate which gives a boost mainly as an integral part of society.

MARRIAGE IN INDIA

In India, according to Hindu Marriage Law, marriage is a sacrament and not a contract. The marriage is considered as a union of two families and not between two individuals.

- Among Hindus, marriage is compulsory. Hindu marriage is based on exogamy.

- Hindus are the only civilized race whose marriage is based on exogamy. Before marriage takes place certain ceremonies must be performed. Only when ***saptapadi*** (seven steps) by the bride and the bridegroom is completed, the marriage becomes legal and binding.
- According to Hindus, marriage is a sacred bond which cannot be dissolved at will. There was no such thing as divorce in Hindu law.
- But later in Hindu Marriage Act of 1955, the right of the woman to divorce her husband has been added. But this freedom is used under certain conditions as stipulated in the law. Although divorce helped many women to lead independent and honorable life, yet it caused instability in the families too. Children are the main victims who suffer because of divorce. So divorce should be granted only when it becomes unavoidable and it is in the interest of both the partners.
- In India, from ancient times women enjoyed a high place in society due to certain historical facts she has come to occupy a lower position. Today again the woman have realized that they are equal to men in every field and there is no need to be subservient to them through the bond of marriage.

SUMMARY

- Marriage, also called matrimony or wedlock, is a socially recognized union between spouses that establishes rights and obligations between them and their respective in-laws.
- Marriage provides the economic cooperation by division of labor among husband and wife or other family members.
- Marriage gatherings help to unite people by certain practices such as rituals before and after marriage.
- In India, according to Hindu Marriage Law, marriage is a sacrament and not a contract.
- Hindus are the only civilized race whose marriage is based on exogamy.
- In Hindu Marriage Act of 1955, the right of the woman to divorce her husband has been added.
- In India, from ancient times women enjoyed a high place in society due to certain historical facts she has come to occupy a lower position.

STUDENT ASSIGNMENT

LONG ANSWER QUESTIONS

1. Describe the forms of marriage.
2. Describe the roles and functions of marriage.
3. Explain the medical and social aspects of marriage.
4. What is marriage and what types of marriages exist?

SHORT ANSWER QUESTIONS

1. Define marriage.
2. Mention the conditions of marriage.
3. Write about any four types of marriage.
4. Write about functions of marriage.
5. Define marriage and its influence on health and health practices.

MULTIPLE CHOICE QUESTIONS

1. Marriage is:

a. A mating relation between male and female
b. A friendly relation
c. Temporary relation
d. None of the above

2. Hindu Marriage Act came into existence from:

a. 1920
b. 1960
c. 1955
d. None of these

3. Marriage by capture is prevalent among the .... tribes of India.

a. Gond
b. Santhal
c. Khasi
d. Jhang

4. **According to traditional Hindu law, marriage is a ....**
   a. Sacrament
   b. Contract
   c. Regulation of prostitution
   d. None of the above

5. **........... is the marriage of a man with the childless widow of his deceased brother.**
   a. Levirate
   b. Sororate
   c. Sororal polygyny
   d. Polygyny

6. **........... may be described as a combination of polygamy and polyandry.**
   a. Monogamy
   b. Levirate
   c. Sororate
   d. Group marriage

7. **Marriage within the caste is known as:**
   a. Endogamy
   b. Exogamy
   c. Incest taboo
   d. Sororate

8. **When after marriage husband lives in the residence of his wife the system is known as:**
   a. Patronymic family
   b. Patriarchal family
   c. Orientation family
   d. Matrilocal residence family

ANSWER KEY

1. a **2.** c **3.** a **4.** a **5.** a **6.** d **7.** a **8.** d

5

Society and Social Groups

LEARNING OBJECTIVES

After the completion of the chapter, the readers will be able to:

- Define society, social group.
- Describe the forms of social groups.
- Understand the characteristics and classification of social groups.
- Explain about group cycle.
- Interpret group morale.

CHAPTER OUTLINE

Society

Meaning

Social Groups

- Social Structure and Social Groups
- Group Cycle
- Group Morale
- Group Behavior

KEY TERMS

Clan: A group of people united by actual or perceived kinship and descent.
Crowd: A large group of people that are gathered or considered together.
Mob: Large crowd of people that may become violent or cause trouble.
Social group: Two or more people who interact with one another, share similar characteristics, and collectively have a sense of unity.
Society: The people in a country or area, thought of as a group, who share customs and laws.

SOCIETY

Society is an integral part of the individual's life from birth to death. The social norms and social values help the individual to have the social identity and the recognition in the society. There are various small and large groups in society as there is continuous human interactions among the individuals in the society. Understanding society, social norms and various social groups helps the nurse to not only understand the society but also helps her to provide the individualistic care to client and also to identify various determinants of health in society.

MEANING

In sociology, the term "society" refers not to a group of people but to the complex pattern of norms of interaction that arises among them. People are important only as agents of social relationships. Some sociologists believe that society exists only when the members know each other and possess common interests or objects.

DEFINITIONS

- "Society is essence pattern, a state or condition, a relationship and therefore necessarily an abstraction." **—Wright**
- "The aggregate of people living together in a more or less ordered community in a particular country or region and having shared customs, laws, and organizations." **—Oxford Dictionary**
- A society is a group of people involved in persistent social interaction and sharing the same geographical or social territory, having the same political authority and culture.

SOCIAL GROUPS

Being in a group is like being empowered and secured. Greek philosopher Aristotle remarks, "Man by nature is a social animal." Group life is essential and inevitable for humans. No man lives in isolation or vacuum. Individuals become humans only in social groups.

DEFINITIONS

- "A social group is given aggregate of people, playing inter-related roles and recognized by themselves or others as a unit of interaction."
  —Williams
- "Social group is a collection of human individuals who are brought into reciprocal relationship." **—MacIver and Page**
- "Groups are aggregates of categories of people who have a consciousness of membership and of interaction." **—Horton and Hunt**
- "A group is a number of people in definable and persisting interaction directed toward common goals and using agreed upon means."
  —Bennett and Tumin
- A social group is a collection of two or more individuals interacting with each other and having common objectives of attention and participate in similar activities.

SOCIAL STRUCTURE AND SOCIAL GROUPS

- The structure of a society affects its rate of change in different ways.
- Social structure is patterned, orderly and enduring form of social relationships that people establish with one another.

Basic Components of Social Structure

There are four basic components of social structure:

1. Status

Status refers to the place or position that a person occupies in a system of social relationship. Within a society a person occupies the status of president of the republic, agricultural labor, son or daughter, violinist, teenager, resident of Nicosia, dentist or neighbor.

A person can hold more than one status simultaneously. For example: Shobhita is an economist, an author, a sister, a resident of India at the same time.

There are three types of status:

i. **Ascribe status:** A social position that is placed on the individual by society, usually on the basis of some inherited characteristics.

ii. **Achieved status:** Attained by a person largely through his/her own effort. One must do something to acquire an achieved status.
iii. **Master status:** A status that dominates others and thereby determines a person's general position within society.

2. Roles

- A role is a set of behaviors typically performed by an individual in a particular social situation. Throughout our lives we are acquiring some social roles. Roles are significant components of our social structure. From a sociological point of view, people could be described as occupying a status but playing a role.
- **Role conflict:** Role conflict occurs when incompatible (clashing, conflicting, opposed) expectations arise from two or more social positions that are held by the same person. In the example given above, the newly promoted director will experience a serious conflict between certain social and occupational roles.

3. Groups

In sociological terms, a group is any number of people with similar norms, values and expectations who regularly and consciously interact. It is important to emphasize that members of a group share same sense of belonging.

Types of Groups

- **Primary and secondary groups:**
  - **Primary group:** It refers to a small group characterized by intimate, face to face association and cooperation.
  - **Secondary group:** It refers to a formal, impersonal group in which there is a little social intimacy or mutual understanding.
- **Comparison between primary and secondary groups is tabulated as:**

Primary group	Secondary group
Generally small	Usually large
Relatively long period of interaction	Short duration
Intimate, face-to-face association	Little social intimacy or mutual understanding
Emotional depth in relationships	Relationships generally superficial
Cooperative, friendly	More formal and impersonal

- **In-groups and out-groups:**
  - An in-group can be defined as any group or category to which people feel they belong to. Simply put, it comprises everyone who is regarded as "we" or "us". The ingroup may be as narrow as one's family or as broad as an entire society.
  - An out-group is a group or category to which people feel they do not belong.
- **Reference groups:**
  - A group that provides an individual with models of how he/she should behave, dress, live.
  - Any group accepted as model or guide for one's judgments or actions. Reference groups have two basic purposes.
    1. They serve a normative function (establishing norms) by setting and enforcing standards of conduct and belief.
    2. Reference groups also perform a comparison function by serving as a standard against which people can measure themselves and others.
- **Social networks:**
  - It is a series of social relationships that link a person directly to others and therefore indirectly to still more people.
  - Involvement in social networks commonly known as networking provides a vital social resource in such tasks as finding employment.

4. Social Institutions

- Social institutions are organized patterns of beliefs and behavior centered on basic social needs.
- The mass media, the government, the economy, the family and the healthcare system are all examples of social institutions.

INTERGROUP RELATIONSHIPS

- Intergroup relationships (relationships between different groups of people) range along a spectrum between tolerance and intolerance.
- The most tolerant form of intergroup relations is pluralism, in which no distinction is made between minority and majority groups, but instead there's equal standing. At the other end of the continuum are:
  - Amalgamation
  - Expulsion
  - Genocide

Special Groups

These are the groups which possess the spatial congruity of its members. For example, clan, tribe, etc.

Tribes and Clans

Differences between tribe and clan are given in Table 5.1.

Tribe

A tribe is collection of the families bearing a common name, speaking a common language, occupying a common territory and is usually not endogamous. Tribes are also referred as wanderers, girijans, etc.

Clan

A clan is a group of individuals who believe themselves as the descendants of a common ancestor real or may by mythical ancestor. Clans are exogamous in nature.
Characteristics of clan:

- Exogamous group
- The members of same clan cannot marry
- They believe in common ancestor
- They are a unilateral group

Crowd

When a large number of people gather at one place it is called crowd, but crowd differs as per the interaction with each other. A crowd is gathering of a considerable number of the persons around a center point of common activities.

TABLE 5.1: Differences between the tribe and clans

Characteristics	Tribes	Clans
Geographical area	Tribes live in a definite geographical area	They do not have a definite geographical area
Language	Language is common	Language is not common
Types of group	Endogamous group	Exogamous group
Classification basis	There can be number of clans in a tribe	Clan is a part of the tribe

Characteristics

- Crowd is anonymous
- It is gathering
- Narrow attention
- Temporary in nature
- Highly influential
- Unity depends upon the interaction among members.

Types of Crowd (Fig. 5.1)

Mob

A mob is defined as "a group of persons stimulating one another to excitement and losing ordinary rational control over their activity, like that of riots."

Audience

"The audience is a form of institutionalized crowd." Audience is crowd formed for a specific period of time based on specific laws.

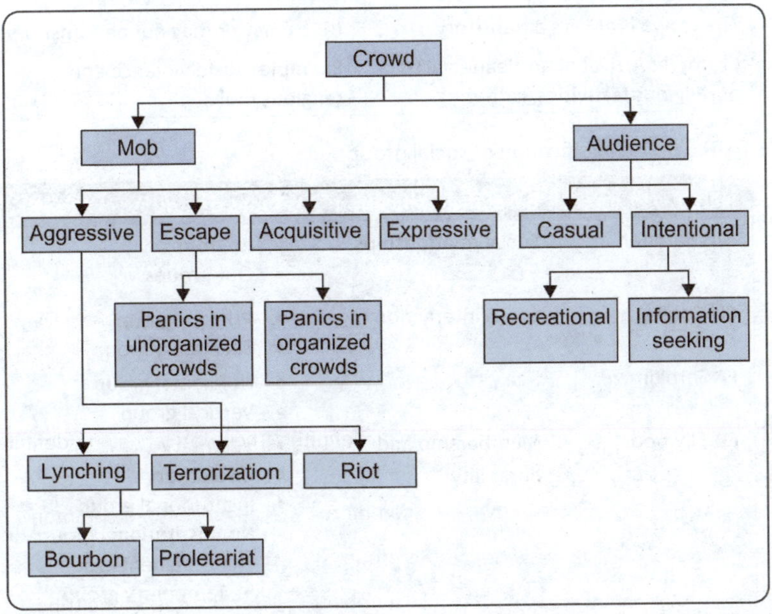

FIGURE 5.1: Types of crowd

Differences between crowd and mob are given in Table 5.2 as follows:

Classification of Social Groups (Table 5.3)

Social groups have been classified in several ways on different basis of classification, by different people. Some of them are as following:

TABLE 5.2: Differences between crowd and mob

Crowd	Mob
Crowd is defined as "a physically compact aggregation of people brought into direct, temporary and unorganized contact with each another."	Mob is defined as "an active crowd that concerns more emotional people, who create problem and do not maintain a peace."
Crowd is anonymous, large and temporary.	Mob is a crowd which has turned in to a violent group, without any well-defined size and characteristics.
Attention of crowd is narrow, may focus on one or two things at a time.	Mob can have multiple attentions at a time.
Crowd easily believe other's words	Mob is a crowd that has gone out of control
The crowd is always a transitory	Mobs may or may not be transitory
Example: Arrival of any leader, actor, or religious festivities/gathering	**Example:** Caste violence and religious mobs

TABLE 5.3: Classification of social groups

Name	Base of classification	Types of groups
WG Sumner	Social relationships	• In-groups • Out-groups
CH Cooley	Social interaction	• Primary group • Secondary group
PA Sorokin	Size	• Horizontal group • Vertical group
CA Ellwood	Membership and durability	• Voluntary • Involuntary • Institutional group
		• Noninstitutional group ▪ Permanent group ▪ Temporary group
Park and Burges	Territory	• Territorial • Nonterritorial

GROUP CYCLE

Just like the human growth cycle, the group cycle is also there. From birth till the death, the man has to be a part of group mostly intentionally or sometimes unintentionally also. Such as, before the birth itself the newborn becomes a family member and later on the birth celebration further introduces the baby with the name of family and also gives an identity to newborn by finalizing the name.

Later on, as the child grows with the family members child has friends and with further growth and development as the child completes the education, gets massy and then again he becomes the part of another family. At this stage, the social circle expands to various formal and the informal groups and further more involvement in social groups happens and this keeps on evolving with the age. The social interactions go on.

GROUP MORALE

Every group irrespective of the origin has certain set code of conduct which explains the expected and unexpected behavior out of the individual in the group. This gives a uniform guideline of human behavior to maintain the uniformity and equality in group. This is usually set by either the leader of the group or collectively by all the members of the group. The group morale is subjected to change anytime depending up on the need of group from time to time.

Significance of the Group Morale

- It provides uniformity to group
- Decreases the biasness among group
- Provides stability to the group
- Prevents frequent clashes among group members
- Improves the strength and communication in the group

GROUP BEHAVIOR

Group behavior is not the individual behavior alone but a whole sum of the members' behavior in a group which reflects the characteristics and nature of the group. This is highly influenced by the behavior of the group members. The different factors such as the individual's attitude, culture, religion and the education affect the group behavior. Individual behavior is the functional aspect of the group behavior. Some of the common factors which influence group behavior are as follows:

- Types of group
- Objectives of group
- Leadership
- Culture and traditions
- Religion

The behavior of individual in group is important, as it gives the social recognition to the group. The good leadership and motivation helps the members to contribute effectively to the group.

SUMMARY

- The social norms and social values help the individual to have the social identity and the recognition in the society.
- In sociology, the term "society" refers not to a group of people but to the complex pattern of norms of interaction that arises among them.
- Social group is a collection of human individuals who are brought into reciprocal relationship.
- Status refers to the place or position that a person occupies in a system of social relationship.
- Role conflict occurs when incompatible (clashing, conflicting, opposed) expectations arise from two or more social positions that are held by the same person.
- In sociological terms, a group is any number of people with similar norms, values and expectations who regularly and consciously interact.
- Involvement in social networks commonly known as networking, provides a vital social resource in such tasks as finding employment.
- Social institutions are organized patterns of beliefs and behavior centered on basic social needs.
- These are the groups which possess the spatial congruity of its members. For example, clan and tribe.
- A crowd is gathering of a considerable number of the persons around a center point of common activities.
- Audience is crowd formed for a specific period of time based on specific laws.
- Social groups have been classified in several ways on different basis of classification, by different people.
- Every group irrespective of the origin has certain set code of conduct which explains the expected and unexpected behavior out of the individual in the group.
- Group behavior is not the individual behavior alone but a whole sum of the members' behavior in a group which reflects the characteristics and nature of the group.

STUDENT ASSIGNMENT

LONG ANSWER QUESTIONS

1. Describe about the society and its types.
2. Explain about the social group and its types.
3. Describe the characteristics of the social group.
4. Explain about group cycle.
5. Describe group morale.
6. What is the difference between tribes and clans?

SHORT ANSWER QUESTIONS

1. Define the following:
   a. Society
   b. Social group
   c. Crowd
   d. Mob
   e. Clan
2. How do social groups form?
3. What factors contribute to the formation of strong social bonds within these groups?
4. Differentiate between primary and secondary social groups with examples of each.
5. List the roles of primary and secondary groups in an individual's life.
6. What is social identity, and how does it influence an individual's sense of belonging and behavior within various social groups?
7. State the role of conflict and cooperation in maintaining group cohesion. Provide examples of how these dynamics shape group interactions.
8. How do social groups contribute to social stability and change within larger societies? Provide examples of how social movements or cultural shifts are influenced by group dynamics.

MULTIPLE CHOICE QUESTIONS

1. **Acceptance in a group is shown ....**
   a. By listening to the group members
   b. Probing and questioning the group members
   c. Solving the problems of the group
   d. Doing things for the group members
2. **Which one of the following is a reference group?**
   a. Occupational group
   b. Group taken to evaluate one's own aspect of life
   c. A relative longer group
   d. A group which allows for social mobility
3. **Social group as a method of social work primarily aims at ....**
   a. Development of leadership qualities
   b. Development of democratic lifestyle
   c. Development of capability for adjustment
   d. All of the above
4. **The main feature of the primary group is ....**
   a. Face to face relationship
   b. Relations are causal
   c. It has large membership
   d. It governs rules and regulations
5. **Which of the following is NOT a primary group?**
   a. Mob
   b. Family
   c. Gang
   d. Peer group
6. **Responsibility for the choice of program in group work rests with ....**
   a. Members of the group
   b. Group worker
   c. The Agency
   d. Members of the group with the help of group worker
7. **Which one of the following is a "secondary group"?**
   a. Nuclear family
   b. Peer group
   c. Association
   d. Joint family

ANSWER KEY

1. a **2.** b **3.** d **4.** a **5.** a **6.** d **7.** c

6

Social Change

LEARNING OBJECTIVES

After the completion of the chapter, the readers will be able to:
- Describe the characteristics and factors affecting social change.
- Explain the role of the nurse in social change.

CHAPTER OUTLINE

- Meaning
- Characteristics of Social Change
- Factors Affecting Social Change
- Role of a Nurse

KEY TERMS

Change: To make radically different.
Social change: The way human interactions and relationships transform cultural and social institutions over time, having a profound impact on society.

Change is a part of life. It is even a sign of growth or also shows that there is no stagnancy. Change is universal and it happens with an individual, family, society or country. Some of the changes are clearly visible but some may not be that evident. Society being dynamic in nature undergoes various changes from time to time.

MEANING

- **Change** is an observable difference or alteration in any phenomenon over a well-defined period of time.
- **Social change** refers to the observable differences in the social phenomenon such as social process and institutional structures or structural arrangements of the society, etc.

DEFINITIONS

- "Social change is, any alterations occur in social organization that is the structure and functions of the society." **—Kingsley Davis**
- "Social change is the change in the social relationships." **—MacIver**
- "Social change means, variations or modifications in any aspect of the social process, pattern or form." **—Dictionary of Sociology**

CHARACTERISTICS OF SOCIAL CHANGE

Social change is:

- Universal phenomenon
- Consists of the modifications or replacements
- Community change
- Not uniform in speed
- Directly related to time
- As essential as a law of nature
- Not predictable
- Not uniform throughout
- Measured in terms of speed of change

FACTORS AFFECTING SOCIAL CHANGE

The social change has occurred in all societies and in all periods of time. But the rate and extent of social change vary with time. There are various factors responsible for social change (Fig. 6.1). These are as follows:

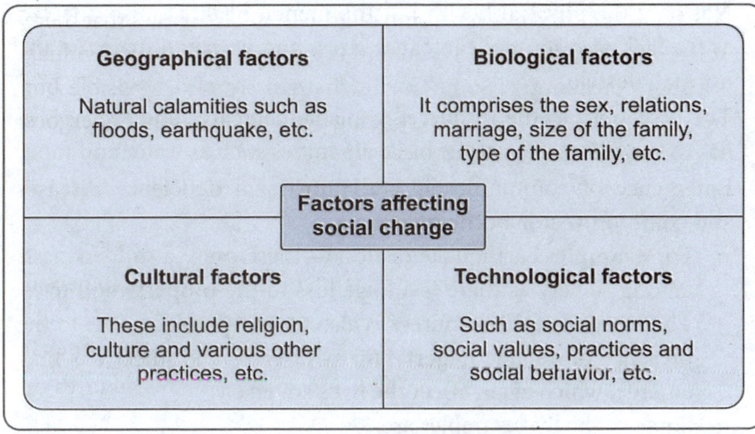

FIGURE 6.1: Factors affecting social change

Geographical Factors/Physical Factors

Changes in the geographical environment cause the changes in society and social life also.

The geographical factors are comprised of all inorganic phenomena which influence human life directly or indirectly.

Some of the geographical factors are as follows:

- Flood
- Earthquake
- Volcano
- Storm
- Famine, etc.

Effects of Geographical Factors on Society and Institution

The change in physical environment sometimes brings out the important changes in the social life because physical environment governs the social life. Every culture that prospers in a definite physical environment limits or permits the growth of civilization.

Every society tries its best to harness its natural resources in its environment. Material and social prosperity of any society and social institute depends mainly on the availability of the natural resources.

The lack of resources affects human lives as following:

- Lack of natural resources affects lives of individuals hence affects the society also.

- Not only the physical health but the mental health is also affected as the lack of resources can cause stress and worry to maintain the normal lifestyle.
- The proximity to the resources available decreases and the person has to travel more to get the basic amenities such as water and food.
- Emergence of communicable and nutritional deficiency diseases and common vector-borne infections.
  - **For example:** Earthquake or flood—these cause a sudden crisis among society as there is a huge loss to the property and lives. The scarcity of the resources is also a basic problem. Due to the presence of organic material many diseases and infections may emerge, which again affect the lives adversely.
  - Some of the live examples are:
    - 2015, Nepal earthquake
    - 2001, Gujarat earthquake
    - 2014, Jammu and Kashmir floods
    - 2013, Uttarakhand floods

Biological Factors

Biological factors bring many changes in the society. Biology involves both quality and quantity of population. The human biological environment includes the factors that determine the numbers, composition, selection and the hereditary qualities of the successive generations.

Human element in the society is always changing. Once we compare the present generation with their parents and grandparents then we know how things are changing grossly. Changes in population have great effect on the society which in turn affects the health of the individual.

- **Natural selection:** The nature selects only those who are strong and efficient.

  Natural selection acts through the death rate. Those who cannot adjust themselves according to the nature, they are killed by the nature. Natural selection works at three levels:
  1. Struggle against nature
  2. Struggle against other species
  3. Struggle within the same species
- **Social selection:** It is the process which creates circumstances that would influence reproduction and survival. Social selection is of two types. They are as follows:

1. **Direct social selection:** In direct social selection, man himself creates social conditions which affect the birth and death rates. For example, modern man adopts family planning and limits the size of the family.
2. **Indirect social selection:** In contrast, in indirect social selection, society creates situations which influence the birth or death rates.

Effects of Biological Factors on Society and Institution

Heredity and the mutations are two most common effects on the society, as these are inevitable and not measurable also. Example is evolution of human beings.

Cultural Factors

Cultural factors greatly influence society. Societies and cultures are closely related to each other and it could be said that the cultural change involves social change also. The common cultural factors are as follows:

- Values
- Attitudes
- Ideas of great men

Cultural-lag

W F Ogburn introduced the concept of cultural-lag to formulate a systemic theory. According to him there are two types of cultures:

1. **Material culture:** It includes all material things like tools, utensils, machines, houses and roads, dams or all the economic goods.
2. **Nonmaterial culture:** It includes religion, education, customs, and government, etc. When the changes take place in the culture, they stimulate nonmaterial aspects. Changes in material culture will affect the structure and functions of nonmaterial aspect of the culture. According to Ogburn, the material culture changes more rapidly than nonmaterial culture. When nonmaterial culture does not adjust with the conditions of material culture, cultural lag takes place. The lag between the material culture and nonmaterial culture is termed as **cultural lag**. This lag is constantly witnessed between a rapidly advancing technology and old elements of believers and rigid social organization.

Influence of the Culture on Society and Institution

The common factors which are influenced by the culture includes the following:

- Attitude, behavior and the personality, i.e., sense of self and society.
- Language as the mode of communication.
- Clothing and the food habits.
- Religion and religious beliefs and customs such as customs of marriage, celebration of festivals.
- Social relationship (it can be family relations, social and religious organizations, or government relations).
- System for education, role of churches, temples, mosques, etc.
- Mental process of behavior.
- Work habits and products. They differ widely from country to country and region to region.

Technological Factors

Technology, society and life are closely interrelated. The technology affects the society in various ways. It influences social institutions and associations. It modifies old order of the society.

Technology touches all aspects of the life of an individual and it also has the short- and long-term effects. The mode of living, thinking and the production underwent a tremendous change.

The process of digitalization is increasing its boundaries all around the globe. With the use of social media and social sites there is one more social world that has emerged beyond limits and here the people from different countries can communicate not only verbally but also communicate too through video chat or other live calling apps.

There is a great advancement in the method of socialization with the use of technology such as smart phones, laptops, palmtops and pagers, etc. Some of the common examples are:

- Use of internet, calling apps and video chat, conferences, etc.
- Various social networking sites such as Facebook, Twitter, Instagram, Pinterest, etc.
- Use of social groups, like WhatsApp, Quora, etc.

Francis Merrill has presented the following pattern of social change based on technology:

- Technological innovations

- Economic institutions
- Social values
- Social institutions

Technological innovations have given rise to economic institution, and economic institution has given rise to the changes in social values gradually. This situation gives rise to social problems. This may be termed as cultural lag too.

Influence of the Technology on Society and Institution

- Good social connectivity around the globe.
- Increased social awareness through mass media and social networking sites.
- Use of technology helps to save time and money both.
- Privacy of social sites is a matter of concern.
- People become more social on social networking sites and eventually they lose direct contact with the social environment and neighbors.
- More of isolation for an individual in personal life.
- Continuous use of the mobile and other gadgets may cause the e-addiction.
- More of stress and vision related issues due to excessive use of screen based technology.
- Posture related musculoskeletal problems due to use of computers, etc.

ROLE OF A NURSE

- Nurses have the potential and the opportunity to act as agents for change for their families, patients and communities by giving health education and role-modeling healthy behavior.
- They act as a role model by being healthy and practice safe health habits—"Healthier nurses are more productive, more alert, and safe practitioners."
- To play effective role of change agent, nurse has to focus on three main roles as a visionary, facilitator and an ideal person.
- Being a visionary, a nurse communicates, advices, coaches and provides feedback to bring change in any health and educational setting.

- Educating people on what change is needed he/she can play the role of an educator as well. He/she should be an ideal person to bring change.
- Helping in problem solving and research. She plays a role of problem solver also.

SUMMARY

- Change is universal and it happens with an individual, family, society or country.
- Social change refers to the observable differences in the social phenomenon such as social process and institutional structures or structural arrangements of the society, etc.
- Changes in the geographical environment cause the changes in society and social life also.
- The change in physical environment sometimes brings out the important changes in the social life because physical environment governs the social life.
- Biological factors bring many changes in the society.
- Changes in population have great effect on the society, which in turn, affects the health of the individual.
- Heredity and the mutations are two most common effects on the society, as these are inevitable and not measurable also.
- Societies and cultures are closely related to each other and it could be said that the cultural change involves social change also.
- There is a great advancement in the method of socialization with the use of technology, such as smart phones, laptops, palmtops and pagers, etc.
- To play effective role of change agent, nurse has to focus on three main roles as a visionary, facilitator and an ideal person.

STUDENT ASSIGNMENT

LONG ANSWER QUESTIONS

1. Describe about social change.
2. Explain about the factors affecting social change.
3. Describe the characteristics of the social group.
4. Explain the effect of social change on society.
5. Explain the role of a nurse in social groups.

SHORT ANSWER QUESTIONS

1. Define social change.
2. What are the key factors that contribute to social change in societies? Provide examples to illustrate your points.
3. How has technology influenced social change in the past century?
4. Mention the positive and negative impacts of technology with examples.

MULTIPLE CHOICE QUESTIONS

1. **Cultural lag:**
   a. Refers to new forms of social disintegration.
   b. Is the adjustment gap between material and non-material culture.
   c. Occurs when the dominant group forces changes upon the subordinate group.
   d. Is society's way of avoiding the social problems that ensue from social change.
2. **Which among the following is not a component of culture?**
   a. Beliefs
   b. Values
   c. Signs
   d. Development

3. **Which of the following is deliberately formed?**
   a. Community
   b. Society
   c. Association
   d. None of the above

4. **According to Ogburn, the rate of change in material culture is:**
   a. The same as that of nonmaterial culture
   b. Faster than that of nonmaterial culture
   c. Slower than that of nonmaterial culture
   d. None of the above

ANSWER KEY

1. b **2.** d **3.** c **4.** b

7

Social Control

LEARNING OBJECTIVES

After the completion of the chapter, the readers will be able to:

- Define social control, social norms.
- Explain the aims of social control.
- Interpret about different types of social control.
- Describe the characteristics and factors affecting social change.
- Explain the role of the nurse in social change.

CHAPTER OUTLINE

- Aims of Social Control
- Types of Social Control
- Norms

KEY TERMS

Social control: The study of the mechanisms, in the form of patterns of pressure, through which society maintains social order and cohesion.
Social norms: The unwritten rules of behavior that are considered acceptable in a group or society.

Society is comprised of a wide variety of the individuals from different cultures, religions, education and languages so there is a need to maintain the stability and harmony among the society. The society needs to control the behavior of the individual in such a way that there is social peace and order. In order to exist and progress, society should exercise certain control measures over its members. Any deviation from the established way is considered dangerous to the welfare of the society. Such control is called "social control".

E A Ross was the first American sociologist to deal with the concept of the "social control" in his famous book "Social Control" in 1901.

DEFINITIONS

- "Social control refers to devices whereby society brings its members into conformity with the accepted standards of the behavior." **—E A Ross**
- "Social control is the way in which entire social order coheres and maintains itself—how it operates as a whole, as a changing equilibrium." **—MacIver**
- "The pattern of pressure which a society exerts to maintain order and establish rules." **—Ogburn and Nimkoff**

AIMS OF SOCIAL CONTROL

The aims of the social control are to:
- Maintain social peace and order
- Control the behavior of the individuals in the society
- Promote the process of socialization
- Reduce the social incidence of social problems
- Maintain social organization

TYPES OF SOCIAL CONTROL

The different types of social control are as follows (Fig. 7.1):
- According to **Kimball Young** social control has been classified in two types:
  i. **Positive control:** It includes the efforts to encourage ideal or accepted behavior such as rewards, encouragement, praise, etc.
  ii. **Negative control:** It includes the efforts to discourage the unwanted behavior like punishment, disapproval, penalty, etc.

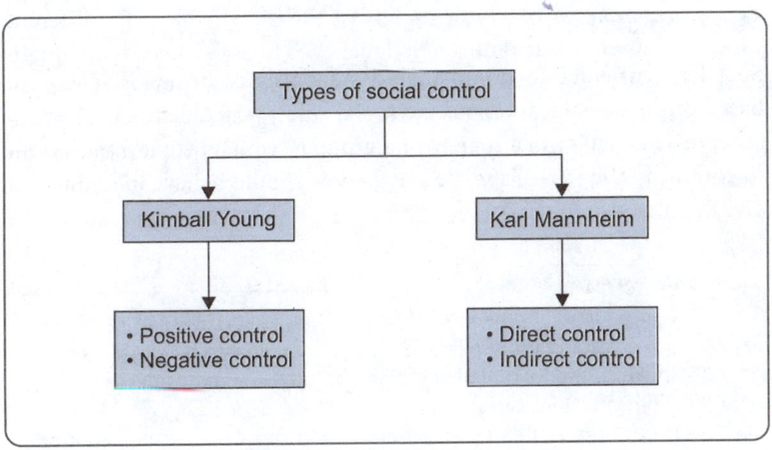

FIGURE 7.1: Types of social control

- According to **Karl Mannheim** social control has been classified in two types:
    i. **Direct control:** The control exerted by the family, neighborhood, village, elders, religious leaders, etc., are the examples of direct control.
    ii. **Indirect control:** The control exerted by the secondary groups or social systems like Folkways, Mores, institutions, public opinions, etc., are the common examples of indirect control.
- The another way of social control is through the **formal and informal** means.
    - Police, courts, law and order comes under the formal means of social control.
    - Informal social controls are those that serve the same purpose of regulating human behavior but are not based on laws. The control being exercised by the customs, Folkways, Mores and religion are the informal means of control.

NORMS

Norms are the standards of the group behavior. Norms help to govern the behavior in the society or it can also be explained as the functional aspect to exercise social control. Norm is a social expectation. It is a standard to which we are expected to confirm that whether we actually do so or not.

Meaning of Norms

Social norms refer to group-shared standards of behavior. These are based on social values. Norms are social rules, which define correct and acceptable behavior in a society or a group to which people are expected to conform. They prescribe the way people should behave in a variety of given situations.

DEFINITIONS

- "A norm is a standard of behavior expectation shared by group members against which the validity of perception is judged and the appropriateness of feeling and behavior is evaluated."
  —Buckman
- "Norms are the standardized generalization concerning expected modes of the behavior."
  —Sheriff and Sheriff

Characteristics of the Social Norms

- Universal
- Nonjudgmental
- Standard of behavior
- Control social conduct
- Relevant to sex, occupation and status
- May or may not be written
- Related to cultural values
- Equal for all the members in the society
- Any violence is strictly not permitted.

Importance of Social Norms

- The norms help to maintain social integrity.
- Norms help to have self-control.
- The norms give a structure to expected behavior in social relationships and interactions.
- To maintain smooth functioning of the society, social norms are essential.
- They help to regulate the behavior of the individuals in the society.
- Norms help to maintain the equality among the society.
- Norms help to influence and motivate the individuals.

Types of Norms

Norms can be classified in different ways but the most important distinction is between prescriptive and proscriptive norms.

- **A prescriptive norm** is positive in form and spells out forms of behavior which role-players are expected to follow means moral values and societal standards norms to be followed.
- **A proscriptive norm** is one which directs a role-player to avoid or abstain from certain type of activity.
- **Formal norms** have generally been written down and involve strict rules for punishment of violators.
  Example: Laws and legal boundaries.
- Informal norms are generally understood but are not precisely recorded.

Means of social control through norms have been depicted in Figure 7.2. Another classification of norms is informal and formal norms.

Informal Norms

Informal norms are generally understood but are not precisely recorded. **Example:** In India, unmarried males and females are not permitted to have any physical relation before marriage that is understood and no one actually explains it but if violated it is not liable to punishment.

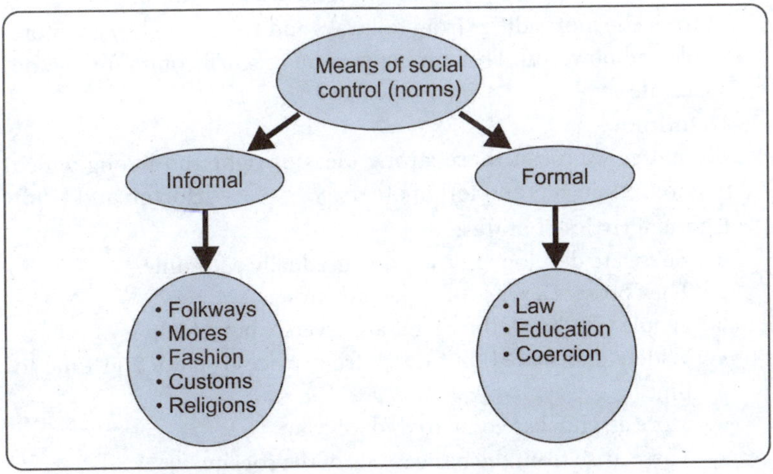

FIGURE 7.2: Means of social control through norms

- **Folkways:** Man is born to fulfill the needs. As there are numerous needs likewise there are different ways also to satisfy those needs. The different measures to meet the needs are tried and then the best out of them is repeated again and again because the needs are satisfied with that method.

  Definitions

  "The folkways are behavioral patterns of everyday life which generally arise unconsciously in a large group." **—Gillin and Gillin**

  "The folkways are the habits of the individual and the customs of the society which arise from efforts to satisfy the needs." **—W G Sumner**

  Characteristics of folkways:
  - These are popular habits or traditions
  - Widely distributed

  No legal punishment, if violated:
  - Less essential as compared to mores
  - Vary from place to place
  - These arise from the efforts to satisfy needs

Differences between folkways and mores are given in Table 7.1.

  Significance of folkways:
  - Folkways help to fulfill the needs of the present and future generations.
  - These help to bring the homogeneity in the social behavior.
  - These are significant in achieving the social control.

- **Mores:** The mores differ from folkways and customs. They are more stable and powerful. These are important in small communities and social life.

  Definition

  "By mores we mean those strong ideas of right and wrong which require certain acts and forbid others." **—Horton and Hunt**

  Characteristics of mores:
  - These are developed slowly and gradually with time.
  - They possess a sense of right and wrong.
  - People who break the mores are severely punished.
  - Widely distributed, but differ from place to place and time to time.
  - More essential as compared to folkways.
  - These arise from the basic needs of the society.

Table 7.1: Differences between the folkways and the mores

Folkways	Mores
The folkways are behavior patterns of everyday life which generally arise unconsciously in a large group	These are strong ideas of right and wrong which require certain acts and forbid others
The examples are—greeting others, proper dressing, etc.	The examples include patriotism, polygamy. It is not permitted as per Hinduism
These explain the basic manners and norms for causal interaction	This explains the right and wrong
Individual is not subjected to punishment, if not followed	Strict punishment is given if violated
These are flexible as per personal choice	These are the social norms and strictly need to be followed
Helpful in showing the courtesy and manners of the society	Helpful in social control

Significance of mores:

- These are essential for social welfare.
- Important element of social control because of associated fear of punishment.
- Mores help to fulfill the needs of the present and future generations.

- **Fashion:** It is an important means of social control as it affects the opinion, beliefs, speech, dress, music, art and craft and literature.

Definition

"Fashions are the folkways that serve for short time period."

—**Lundberg**

Characteristics of fashion:

- Influenced by the choice of group
- Changeable

May change as per place and time:

- All the people may not follow it
- Distribution depends upon the acceptability
- Least essential as compared to folkways and mores.

Differences between fashion and customs are given in Table 7.2.

- **Customs:** Customs are found in all societies and they differ widely from place to place, time to time and community to community also. These are important in less evolved communities.

Table 7.2: Differences between the customs and the fashions

Customs	Fashions
The customs are the practices continued from generation to generation with a degree of formal recognition	Fashion is socially approved sequence of variation on a customary theme
The examples are—caste system and child marriage, dowry system, etc.	The example is trend of frock suits is old but now a days again its being liked by community
These are enduring	It is changeable and shot lived
These are spontaneous	Fashion is changeable
Customs stand	Fashion for individuality
Custom can be broken for sociality	Fashion keeps growing in different arenas

Definition

"Customs are the ways or methods of acting sanctioned and recognized by society."

—MacIver and Page

Characteristics of customs:

- These are traditional
- It is written code of the behavior
- Folkways are influenced by the choice of group
- Not changeable, more rigid and may need more time to change
- All the people follow customs due to fear of punishment.

- **Religion:** Religion is a system of belief and ritual, good behavior and good character forms the basis of the dharma.

Definition

"Religion is the attitude towards superhuman powers."

—Ogburn and Nimkoff

Characteristics of religion:

- These are based on beliefs in supernatural powers.
- Certain acts are classified as sinful.
- It is a way for salvation or mukti.
- It can explain the facts like life after death.
- Religion enhances the self-esteem.
- Religion is a source of social cohesion.
- All the people follow one or the other religion to have a sense of satisfaction and protection.

India is a country with variety of religions but still there is unity as "we Indians."

Formal Norms

Formal norms are generally written down and involve strict rules for punishment of violators.

Example: Laws and legal boundaries

- **Laws:** Laws are confined to modern societies. In ancient society customs, traditions and folkways were sufficient agencies for the social control. But in modern societies these are not that effective hence the strict enforcement of the law is needed.

  Definition

  "Law is the body of rules which are recognized, interpreted and applied to particular situation by the court of the land."—**MacIver and Page**

  Characteristics of law:

  - It is a body of rules and regulations
  - It is the best way of social control
  - Laws are made by state or political power
  - Laws are uniform for a nation throughout
  - There is strict punishment for the violation of law
  - The decisions are taken by the judiciary system only.
- **Education:**
  - Education is the process by which there is significant change in the behavior, knowledge and attitude of an individual.
  - Education is a process of the socialization. It helps a child to prepare as per the society requirements.
  - It is the most powerful way to shape the future of the nation or to bring the change.
  - It helps to decrease various deeply rooted social problems very easily.
  - It changes the mindset and thinking of an individual from the community and culture he belongs to, up till the national or international platform.
  - The education plays a key role in social change.
- **Coercion:**
  - The use of force and power to achieve a desired end is called the coercion.
  - It may be physical or nonviolent also.

  - It is the ultimate way to extend social control when all the other ways of social control fails.
  - The physical coercion may take the form of the death penalty or imprisonment also.
  - It is the lowest form of social control.
  - The nonviolence ways include strike, boycott and non-cooperation. It is a successful way of social control. The best example is "Mahatma Gandhi used it against the Britishers."
- **Politics and social control:**
  - Politics is another very powerful tool for social control.
  - The various other tools such as parliamentary institutions, administrative powers, the policy making and governance also help to control the society.
  - Politics is divided into elements of control one is state and second is central government. Both function at different levels to maintain the social harmony by revising and forming the social norms and policies. Example: Swachh Bharat Abhiyan.

SUMMARY

- The society needs to control the behavior of the individual in such a way that there is social peace and order.
- Police, courts, law and order come under the formal means of social control.
- Informal social controls are those that serve the same purpose of regulating human behavior but are not based on laws.
- Norms help to govern the behavior in the society or it can also be explained as the functional aspect to exercise social control.
- Norms are the standardized generalization concerning expected modes of the behavior.
- The folkways are behavioral patterns of everyday life which generally arise unconsciously in a large group.
- Folkways help to fulfil the needs of the present and future generations.
- Mores are important in small communities and social life. These are strong ideas of right and wrong which require certain acts.
- Customs are the ways or methods of acting, sanctioned and recognized by society.
- Formal norms are generally written down and involve strict rules for punishment of violators.
- Education is the process by which there is significant change in the behavior, knowledge and attitude of an individual.
- The use of force and power to achieve a desired end is called the coercion.
- Politics is divided into elements of control one is state and the other is central government.

STUDENT ASSIGNMENT

LONG ANSWER QUESTIONS

1. Explain social control and the role of various agencies for social control.
2. Enlist the aims of social control.
3. Describe the types of norms.
4. Explain the importance of norms in social control.
5. Differentiate between folkways and mores.
6. Differentiate between customs and fashion.
7. Describe the role of politics in social control.

SHORT ANSWER QUESTIONS

1. Define the following:
   a. Social control
   b. Norms
   c. Mores
   d. Folkways
   e. Law
   f. Custom
   g. Fashion
   h. Religion
2. What is social control and what are its primary functions in maintaining social order within communities and societies?
3. What are the different forms of social control, including informal and formal mechanisms? Provide examples of each.
4. Who are the agents responsible for exerting social control within a society? How do these agents enforce norms and regulate behavior?
5. How does social control respond to deviant behavior?
6. What is the role of sanctions and stigma in regulating and discouraging deviance?

MULTIPLE CHOICE QUESTIONS

1. **The term "control" involves:**
   a. The idea of restraint or direction
   b. Overtone to a culture
   c. System of land reforms

2. **Which of the following is not true about term "control"?**
   a. The idea of restraint or direction
   b. Process or technique of control
   c. It stands on the way of democracy
   d. None of the above

3. **Which of the following is true about social control?**
   a. The idea of restraint and direction
   b. Includes formal and informal mode which has an impact on others
   c. Both a and b
   d. None of the above

4. **Ultimate basis of social control is:**
   a. Social organization
   b. Social mobility
   c. Social class
   d. None of these

5. **In our modern times:**
   a. Every society is exclusively competitive
   b. No society is either exclusively competitive or exclusively cooperative
   c. Every society is exclusively cooperative
   d. None of the above

6. **A norm is a:**
   a. Specific guide to action
   b. Culture of society
   c. Guideline for socialization
   d. Guideline for social interaction

7. **Norms are enforced by:**
   a. Positive sanction
   b. Negative sanction
   c. Order
   d. Positive and negative sanction

8. **Norms are imposed through .... means of social control.**
   a. Formal and legal
   b. Formal and informal
   c. Cultural
   d. Informal and legal

9. **A value is a belief that is:**
   a. Moral
   b. Very productive in society
   c. Good and desirable
   d. Cultural

ANSWER KEY

1. a **2.** c **3.** c **4.** a **5.** b **6.** a **7.** d **8.** b **9.** c

8

Social Stratification

LEARNING OBJECTIVES

After the completion of the chapter, the readers will be able to:

- Define social stratification.
- Describe the characteristics and functions of social stratification.
- Explain the various forms of social stratification.
- Discuss the caste and class system.
- Describe social mobility.

CHAPTER OUTLINE

- Characteristics of Social Stratification
- Functions of Social Stratification
- Forms of Social Stratification
- Social Mobility

KEY TERMS

Caste: A system in which people are born into their social standing and will remain in it their whole lives.

Class: A group of people within a society who possess the same socioeconomic status.

Social mobility: Shift in an individual's social status from one status to another.

Social stratification: A society's categorization of its people into groups based on socioeconomic factors like wealth, income, race, education, ethnicity, gender, occupation, social status, or derived power.

The society is one unit but again it has certain subunits in which there is ranking of the different categories of people in a hierarchy. This system divides individuals into strata that is called the social stratification. Each and every society is divided into different groups. It is even seen in most primitive societies. Stratification involves the distribution of unequal rights and privileges among the different members of a society. Social stratification means division of society into social classes, caste and other divisions.

Difference is the law of nature. Every society is divided in one way or the other. No two individuals are exactly alike. Diversity and variety are inherent in every society. That is why human society is stratified everywhere.

There are different views for the concept of social stratification, it has been defined differently by different sociologists.

DEFINITIONS

- "The process by which the individuals and groups are ranked more or less enduring hierarchy of status is known as stratification."
  —Ogburn and Nimkoff
- "Social stratification is horizontal division of society into higher and lower social units." **—R W Mury**
- "Unstratified society with real equality of its members is a myth, that can never be realized in the history of mankind." **—P A Sorokin**

CHARACTERISTICS OF SOCIAL STRATIFICATION

According to **M M Tumin,** the important characteristics of social stratification are as following: Social stratification is:

- **A social phenomenon:** Biological traits do not determine social superiority and inferiority by the time they are socially recognized. **Example:** The principal of school attains a dominant position not by physical strength, age but by possessing the socially defined traits. Education, training, skills, experience, and personality, etc., are more important than one's biological equalities.
- **Universal:** The stratification system is a universal phenomenon. Difference between rich and poor is found everywhere. There is no society that is unstratified.

- **Ancient:** The stratification system is not a new phenomenon. It is very old. According to historians, stratification exists even in small wandering groups. Difference between the rich and the poor, royal family member and common villagers—it existed among all societies and tribes.
- **Diversity:** Stratification is not same for all societies. It is different from one society to another society. Class and caste are the general forms of stratification found even in modern world.
- Stratification has consequences such as:
    - **Life chances:** It means things such as neonatal mortality, physical and mental illness, longevity, childlessness and divorce, etc. Life chances are involuntary.
    - **Lifestyles:** It includes mode of housing, education, leisure time, type of relationship between the parents and children, and so on. Lifestyle shows differences in preferences, priorities, tastes, and values.

FUNCTIONS OF SOCIAL STRATIFICATION

- The social stratification is graded into division of prestige and power.
- It provides the placement and motivation of individuals in order to affect the performance of their social duties.
- It facilitates a system of rewards to members for carrying out various duties associated with different positions. The reward also can be monetary or nonmonetary like prestige and positions.
- The organization of societies into hierarchy of social status helps to obtain the performance of functions needed to operate a society properly.
- Stratification distinguishes the various positions of a society in a hierarchy of status that regulates the relationship between the people within a society.

FORMS OF SOCIAL STRATIFICATION

Stratification is universal but expresses itself in diverse forms. The Hindu caste system is also considered as a form of social stratification. Other forms of stratification such as slavery, estates, caste system, class system, etc., are briefly discussed ahead. The caste system focused on the differences between the *"open"* class system and the *"closed"* caste system.

Caste System

The word **Caste** is the Spanish word **Casta** which means breed, race or a complex system of hereditary traits. The Portuguese used this term to the class of people in India commonly known by the name of **Jati**. The English word caste is an adjustment of the original term.

DEFINITIONS

- "When a class is somewhat strictly hereditary we may call it as "caste."
  —C H Cooley
- "A caste is a closed group." **—Mazumdar**
- A caste is a group having two basic characteristics:
  - Membership is confined to those who are born of members and includes all persons so born,
  - The members are forbidden by an inexorable social law to marry outside the group. **—Ketkar**

Origin of Caste System

Many Western and Indian scholars have described the origin of castes in their own ways, some important theories are given as follows:

- **Traditional theory:** This theory owes its origin to the ancient literature. This theory believes that caste has a divine origin. There are some references in the Vedic literature, wherein it is said that castes were created by Brahma, the supreme creator. He created different castes for the harmonious performance of various social functions for the maintenance of society. According to the *"Purushasukta"* hymn of the Rig Veda, the Brahmanas are supposed to have born from the mouth of the Supreme Being, the *Kshatriya* from the arms, the *Vaishya* from the thighs and the *Sudra* from the feet of the creator.
- **Theory of cultural integration:** This theory has been propounded by Sarat Chandra Roy. Roy has the opinion that caste is an outcome of the interaction between the Indo-Aryans varna system on the one hand and the tribal system of the *Dravidian* on the other. Thus, Sarat Chandra Roy holds that caste system evolved as a result of integration and assimilation of different cultures like the Aryan's *"Karma"* based varna system and the tribal system of the Dravidian

occupational division of society, etc. As the number of ethnic groups increased, the caste system began to grow more complex.

- **Occupational theory:** Nesfield considered caste system as the natural product of the occupational division of Hindu society. In his own words, "Function and function alone is responsible for the origin of caste system." He holds the view that in the beginning when there was no rigidity, each individual was free to have occupation of his choice. But slowly and gradually with the rigidity in the system, occupational changes came to a halt. Castes were identified on the basis of fixed occupation. Persons in noble occupations, such as educating the people, fighting in the battlefield, trade, etc., were considered as members of superior castes.
- **Political theory:** Some scholars have the opinion that not race but political convenience and manipulation by those who wish to retain authority, resulted in the origin of caste system. The Brahmins were solely responsible for creating and maintaining this system so as to relish authority.
- **Racial theory of caste:** Herbert Risley cited the racial theory of the origin of caste system. According to this theory, caste system came into existence due to clash of cultures and the contact of races. The Aryans came to India as conquerors, because of their better complexion, physical appearance and good physique, in comparison to the non-Aryans. The Aryans placed themselves as a superior race over the non-Aryans.

  Thus the Aryans considered the natives as inferior to them and maintained their own ideas and ceremonial purity. The Aryans got married to the non-Aryan women, but refused to give their own daughters in marriage to the non-Aryans. The offsprings born out of such marriages were called the **Chandal**. The **Chandalas** had the lowest position in society. Thus, the irregular unions between races and racial superiority were held responsible for the origin of caste system in India.
- **Evolutionary theory: Denzil Ibbetson** has presented this evolutionary theory of origin of caste system. The theory implies that the caste system did not come into existence all of a sudden. It is the consequence of social evolution. The caste system has emerged slowly and gradually. The factors, which contributed to it, included

desire for purity of blood, devotion to a particular profession, theory of Karma, conquests of one army by the other, geographical location and isolation.

Process of Development of Caste System

Herbert Risley has mentioned six processes of development of caste system.

1. **Change in traditional occupation:** When a caste or a sub-caste changes its traditional occupation and adopts a different one. It ultimately develops into a distinct caste.
2. **Migration:** In the past, the transport and communication system were not developed. Therefore, whenever a section of caste migrated from one region to the other, it faced difficulties in maintaining contacts with the earlier place. In course of time, it was linked with the parental caste.
3. **Customary changes:** From the earliest times, the formation of new castes was based on the rejection of old custom and usages and acceptance of the new practices and habits.
4. **Preservation of old practices:** Some caste groups are interested in maintaining their old traditions and on their bases they separated themselves from the rest of society who followed relatively new customs and traditions. The caste groups preserving old patterns may take up new names. This resulted in the formation of new castes.
5. **Getting into the folds of Hinduism:** Certain tribes or the section of the tribes enter into the rank on Hinduism by:
    - Changing their lineage
    - By accepting the tenets of any school of Hindu religion
    - By joining Hindu religion
    - By establishing relations with the Hindus without changing its name.
6. **Role of religious enthusiasts:** Separate sects are created by the religious enthusiasts. They preach their doctrines and attract people toward them. Gradually their followers developed as a new group. Kabir may be taken as an example in this context.

Do you know?

Varna and Caste

The terms **varna** and **caste** are used interchangeably. But it is misleading as **varna** may be defined as abstract classification of persons on the basis of mythical origin (Table 8.1).

Table 8.1: Differences between varna and caste

Varna	Caste
Literally Varna means color and it is originated from the word ***"Vri"*** meaning the choice of one's occupation. Hence, ***varna*** is concerned with one's color or occupation	Caste or ***"Jati"*** originated from the Sanskrit word ***"Jana"*** which implies taking birth. Thus, caste is concerned with birth
Varnas are only four in number that is Brahmin, Kshatriya, Vaishya, and Sudra	Castes are very large in number. Castes also have many subdivisions commonly known as sub castes
It is a national phenomenon	There are different regional variations based on linguistic differences
The hierarchical pattern of ***varna*** shows the concept of purity and pollution as the basis of division of society and placements of groups into higher and lower classes, i.e., ***varna*** class correlation are mostly positive	Caste-class correlation is not always positive; there may be variations in the placement due to economic, political, and educational status of various groups

Characteristics of Caste

Some of the important features of caste are as following:

- **Segmental division of the society:** The society is divided into various castes with a well-developed life of their own, the membership of which is determined by the consideration of birth. The status of a person does not depend on his wealth but on the traditional importance of the caste in which he had the fortune of being born. Caste is hereditary, and there is no provision to change caste status. Status is determined not by vocation but by birth.
- **Hierarchy of status:** Each caste has a customary name that helps to set it apart. The whole society is divided into distinct classes.

Brahmins in India stand at the top of the social ladder and the **Sudras** come under the bottom of the caste hierarchy of social status.

- **Food-related restrictions:** Another element of caste system is the complex system of "tabs" by which the superior castes try to preserve the ceremonial purity. There are certain restrictions on food habits. Social intercourse and minute rules are laid down with regard to the kind of food that can be acceptable by a person and from which caste. For example, a **Brahmin** will accept **pakka** food, (food prepared in **ghee** and milk) from any community. But he cannot accept **kachcha food** (prepared out of water) from the hands of other castes.
- **Marital restraints:** A person born in a caste remains in that caste throughout his life. Every caste is subdivided into sub-caste. Every caste forbids its members to marry persons outside it. Thus, each subcaste is endogamous. This principle of endogamy is so strict; any person violating this law is expelled out of his own subcaste.
- **Restrictions related to occupation:** Members of a particular caste are expected to follow the caste occupation. They cannot change their occupations. The abandonment of hereditary occupation is not considered as right. No caste would allow its members to take up any degraded occupations. It was not only the moral restraint of one's occupation but also the restrictions put by other castes whose members did not allow members of the caste other than their own to follow their occupation. Thus, any one not born as a **Brahmin** was not allowed to function as a priest.
- **Social and religious disabilities:** In the traditional caste society, lower caste people suffered certain social and religious disabilities. Even today, at many places Sudras are not allowed to draw water from public wells. During the early days, public places like hotels, hostels, public lecture halls, temples, schools were not kept open for the lower caste people particularly the Dalits. Entrance to temple and other places of religious importance were forbidden for them.

Roles of Caste

The positive and negative roles of caste system are as follows:

Positive Role

- **A definite social environment** is provided to its members. Cultural values and practices of each caste are different from the other.

Thus, caste system makes one's life happier by providing a fixed social environment.

- **Unity:** Caste system promotes creation among its members. There is a sense of we feeling among the members of the caste. It is because of this spirit creation is automatically developed.
- **Economics:** Caste system determines the occupation of its members. The children are given training by the parents and other elder members of their caste to earn their livelihood for economic stability.
- **Racial purity:** Caste system maintains social purity by prohibiting inter caste marriages.
- **Separate social and political lives:** Caste system separates social life from political influence. Many invaders of our country like the Muslims and Christian people always try to convert Hindus into their own religion. But caste system abstracts such efforts.

Negative Role

- **Least scope for social mobility:** The caste system does not encourage mobility of labor. It provides limited opportunity to change their social status.
- **Untouchability:** It is a dark spot on the face of Hinduism. Caste hierarchy leads to the feelings of superiority and also untouchability. Persons of higher caste presume that even the touch of a **shudra** will pollute them. They are treated as subhuman. Dalits have suffered from many social disabilities and were forbidden from public places such as temples, hotels and public wells.
- **Social disunity:** Caste system has been divided into thousands of subcaste groups. This has developed hatredness and enmity among the members and that replaced the feelings of respect and sympathy among the members of higher and lower caste.
- **Inappropriate occupation placement:** In caste system, some specific occupations are allotted a particular caste. The members of one caste are forbidden to take an occupation allotted to another caste. This has placed a wrong man in wrong occupation.
- **Hindrance of national unity:** A modern nation can become strong only by following the principles of liberty, equality and fraternity. But caste system is exactly opposite to it. It has provided a great interest in the national integration.

- **A scope for religious conversion:** The lower caste people are getting themselves converted to Islam and Christianity, due to the brutality of the upper caste.

Disintegration of Caste System in India

The causes of disintegration of caste system are following:

- **Modern education:** The religious education encourages the caste system but modern education traces the ideas of liberty, equality and fraternity. Education has encouraged intercaste marriages. Young generations are free from the feelings of superiority and untouchability. So modern education is one of the factors that is not favorable to caste system.
- **Globalization:** The use of technology around the globe has a great effect on the caste system as there is a mutual interaction among different individuals from different countries and religions. This helps to decrease the discrimination on the basis of caste. Thus, the base of the caste system began to lose its importance in the modern era.
- **Economy:** In the earlier time, power of money was not considered as a dominant factor. People were more concerned about their spiritual and religious attainments. But in the modern age wealth determines the social status not the caste system. Nowadays, a person takes up a profession which is most profitable. Today a wealthy **Shudra** is more respected than a poor **Brahmin**. Here, the caste system is abolished because of respect toward status in society.
- **Class system:** The class system is replacing the ancient caste system. As the class consciousness grows stronger, caste consciousness is vanishing away.
- **Legal system:** In the present era all the members of the society are subjected to the same lane irrespective of caste. Due to this the caste **panchayat** lost their powers and social status. The law is above all and everyone has a faith that the decision by the judiciary system is the final.
- **Democracy:** Democracy which is introduced by the Indian constitution treats all alike before the lane. The caste system is against the principles of democracy.

Class System

Class is a group of people sharing the same social status with respect to certain characteristics. These characteristics are not given by birth usually but are acquired through individual efforts in the course of life.

DEFINITIONS

- "A social class is a culturally defined group that is accorded a particular position or status within the population as a whole". **—Lapiere**
- "A social class is a portion of community marked off from the rest by social status". **—MacIver**
- "A social class is the aggregation of persons having essentially the same social status in a given society". **—Ogburn and Nimkoff**

Characteristics of Class System

Class system is a system of social stratification and is almost universal.

- **Hierarchy:** Unlike the caste system, class system also has a hierarchical order in relation to each other.
- **Open system:** Class is an open system, because a person can change his status by putting efforts.
- **Class is an acquired trait:** It is not based on birth like the caste but is achieved by individual qualities.
- **Common way of living:** People of some social class have usually a common way of living and this may differentiate them from other classes.
- **Determination of social status:** A person's social status is more or less determined by the class to which he belongs.
- **Opportunities:** Class system opens free opportunities to upgrade in life. Class may be determined on the basis of several criteria as mentioned below:
  - On the basis of mode of earning livelihood:
    - Business class
    - Professional class
    - Labor class

Table 8.2: Differences between caste and class

Caste	Class
Specific: The caste system is unique to India, hence it is not universal	**Universal:** The class system is universal in nature
Criteria for classification: Birth is the criteria of the status and not the achievement	**Acquired status:** Status is achieved by the individual
Closed system: Caste system is a closed system. It restricts social mobility	**Open system:** It facilitates social mobility. Individuals can move from the lower class to the upper class
Endogamous group: A caste member has to marry within the group, select the life partner from his own caste system. Intercaste marriages are not permitted	**Exogamous group:** The members are free to select their life partner from any one of the classes
Origin: The caste system is believed to have a divine origin. It is based on Hindu traditions	**Secular:** The class system is secular. It has nothing to do with religion

- On the basis of economic status:
  - Upper class
  - Middle class
  - Lower class
- On the basis of educational status:
  - Uneducated
  - Less educated
  - Educated

Differences between caste and class are given in Table 8.2.

SOCIAL MOBILITY

The movement of people or group of people from one social status or position to another status or position within a society is known as social mobility. For example, the poor people may become rich, a shopkeeper may become a big businessman, a common man may become prime minister and so on. At the same time, a business tycoon may become bankrupt, rich man may become poor and so on.

Types of Social Mobility

- **Vertical social mobility:** The movement of group of people from one social status to another is known as vertical mobility. It involves change in class, occupation and power. Vertical mobility may be upward or downward both.
- **Downward social mobility:** The movement of a person or a group from upper to lower social class is called as downward mobility. For example, a politician may become a bankrupt.
- **Upward social mobility:** The movement of a person or a group from the lower class to upper class. For example, a clerk becomes a bank manager; a farmer becomes a minister, etc.
- **Horizontal social mobility:** It indicates a change in position, without the change of status. For example, a nursing officer working in a hospital may resign from the job and join another hospital as a nursing officer and work in more or less the same capacity.

Factors Influencing Social Mobility

The following are the factors influencing social mobility:

- **Motivation:** The driving force behind actions is called motivation. Each individual has a desire not only to have a better way of living but also wants to improve his social status.

  Example: People from villages migrate to cities in search of new job.
- **Education:** Education not only helps an individual to acquire knowledge but is also a permit for the professional career. It is only after acquiring minimum formal education that individual can aspire to occupy higher positions.

  Example: Students with families migrate from villages to cities in order to avail better educational qualifications.
- **Skill training:** Skill training is the area in which our country is focusing, the basic skill training not only helps the individual to earn money but it also decreases the unemployment. The quality of work is greatly improved with the skill training. In other words, skills training facilitates improvement of the position, leading to social mobility.

  Example: Skill training for disaster management and basic life support.

- **Migration:** A particular place may not have opportunities and facilities to improve upon. Therefore, people are compelled to migrate to other places to earn their livelihood.
  Example: People belonging to Uttar Pradesh and Bihar, migrate to the States of Punjab and Haryana to earn their livelihood. Here they become farm laborers. After accumulating money, they go back to their villages and buy lands.
- **Industrialization:** This is an era of industrialization, after acquiring the new vocational training people can get jobs in industries. With experience, they can move up in the social ladder. In the industrial society, the statuses are achieved, whereas in the traditional society like India, the statuses are ascribed according to birth. Hence, industrialization facilitates greater social mobility.
  Example: Traditional occupation is now replaced with the family business, when a farmer shifts work from agriculture to seed industry.
- **Urbanization:** If an individual has higher education, good income and is engaged in occupation of higher prestige, he occupies high social status irrespective of his caste. Urbanization facilitates social mobility by removing the factors which hinder social mobility.
  Example: People who belong to schedule caste can become IAS officers with good education, that is how the traditional caste related practices are abolished nowadays.
- **Legislation:** The enactment of new laws can also facilitate social mobility. The legal provision for reservation of jobs and promotion for the scheduled castes and scheduled tribes has also helped in social mobility.
  Example: When Zamindari Abolition Act was passed, most of the tenant cultivators became owner cultivators which indicates improvement in their status, i.e., from tenants to owner cultivators. Similarly, Hindu Marriage Act in different ways has enhanced the status of women. Similarly, Hindu Succession Act has given equal rights to the daughter in the family property.
- **Modernization:** The process of modernization involves use of scientific knowledge and latest technology. It also refers to rationality and secular way of life.
  Example: With the improvement in technology, people engaged in occupations of low prestige like sanitary staff discard their traditional occupations and take up other prestigious occupations.

The social stratification continued in the past as caste system and continues in present as class system. It divides the society in different levels of hierarchy on the basis of different criteria. The present society welcomes the change as it comes.

SUMMARY

- Social stratification means division of society into social classes, caste and other divisions.
- There are different views for the concept of social stratification, it has been defined differently by different sociologists.
- Biological traits do not determine social superiority and inferiority by the time they are socially recognized.
- Stratification distinguishes the various positions of a society in a hierarchy of status that regulates the relationship between the people within a society.
- The word Caste is the Spanish word Casta which means breed, race or a complex system of hereditary traits.
- Caste is hereditary, and there is no provision to change caste status.
- Social intercourse is communication between people as they spend time together.
- Every caste forbids its members to marry persons outside it.
- The abandonment of hereditary occupation is not considered right.
- Caste system separates social life from political influence.
- Caste hierarchy leads to the feelings of superiority and also untouchability.
- The lower caste people are getting themselves converted to Islam and Christianity, due to the brutality of the upper caste.
- So, modern education is one of the factors that is not favorable to caste system.
- The caste system is against the principles of democracy.
- Class is a group of people sharing the same social status with respect to certain characteristics.
- Class system is a system of social stratification and is almost universal.
- The movement of people or group of people from one social status or position to another status or position within a society is known as social mobility.
- The basic skill training not only helps the individual to earn money but it also decreases the unemployment.
- The social stratification continued in the past as caste system and continues in present as class system.

STUDENT ASSIGNMENT

LONG ANSWER QUESTIONS

1. Describe social stratification.
2. Enlist the characteristics and functions of social stratification.
3. Explain in detail about:
   a. Class system
   b. Caste system
4. Differentiate between:
   a. Class and caste
   b. Positive and negative caste system
   c. Varna and caste
5. Describe about social mobility.

SHORT ANSWER QUESTIONS

1. Define the following:
   a. Social stratification
   b. Class
   c. Caste
   d. Social mobility
2. How does social class influence an individual's access to education, healthcare, and career opportunities? Provide examples to support your answer.
3. Mention the factors contributing to gender stratification in societies.
4. What are some of the consequences of gender inequality for individuals and communities?
5. Compare and contrast the concepts of meritocracy and social inheritance in relation to social stratification.
6. How do social stratification vary across different global regions?
7. What are some common patterns and disparities observed in wealth distribution and social status worldwide?

MULTIPLE CHOICE QUESTIONS

1. **Social stratification is:**
   a. A system in which people can change their status with relative ease
   b. Based entirely on self-classification
   c. The ranking or grading of individuals and groups into hierarchical layers
   d. None of the above

2. **The process of movement of people of group from one social status to another is called as:**

a. Movement
b. Social differentiation
c. Social stratification
d. Social mobility

3. **Which of the following is not a major cause of social stratification?**

a. Social tensions
b. Absence of change in social values
c. Natural calamities
d. All of the above

4. **Division of society on the basis of class is:**

a. Peculiar to few affluent societies
b. Of comparatively recent origin
c. Found in all societies since times past
d. All of the above

5. **A social class is a portion of community marked off from the rest by social status is defined by:**

a. Maclver and Page
b. Ogburn
c. Nimkoff
d. None of these

6. **Which one of the following is not true of social class?**

a. The members are quite ready to give up their privileges
b. The members have external unity
c. The members have no external unity
d. None of the above

7. **Which one of the following does not fit in the characteristic of social class?**

a. Each class has certain privileges
b. It represents vertical division of society
c. Social class comes into being due to social stratification
d. None of the above

ANSWER KEY

1. c **2.** d **3.** b **4.** c **5.** a **6.** a **7.** b

Notes

9

Social Problems

LEARNING OBJECTIVES

After the completion of the chapter, the readers will be able to:

- Define social control and social norms.
- Explain the aims of social control.
- Describe different types of social control.
- Analyze the characteristics and factors affecting social change.
- Explain the role of the nurse in social change.

CHAPTER OUTLINE

- Prostitution
- Crime
- Divorce
- Dowry
- Juvenile Delinquency
- Drug Abuse and Drug Addiction
- Alcoholism
- Handicapped or Disability
- Population
- Slums
- Social Agencies and Remedial Measures

KEY TERMS

Social agencies: A private or governmental organization that provides personal services, especially in the field of health and welfare.

Social problems: Any condition or behavior which has negative consequences for large number of people.

Life is process of continuous adjustment. When various parts of the society are well-adjusted, we get an organized society. Social problems are the behavior pattern or situations that are considered objectionable or undesirable in society. The social problems disturb the harmony and peace of society. There are a number of social problems but the extent and type of problems may vary from one community to another. Some common examples such as dowry system, prostitution, drug addiction, alcoholism, juvenile delinquency, child abuse, population explosion, corruption, poverty, unemployment and sexual deviance, etc., are considered as major social problems.

DEFINITIONS

- "A condition where there is deviation from social norms."
  —Fuller and Myers
- "A condition affecting significant number of people in ways considered undesirable; about which it is felt that something can be done through or the collective social action." **—Horton and Leslie**

PROSTITUTION

This is an ambiguous term which is not simple to define. But the simplest definition says that "it is an exchange of money for sexual purpose that is offering sexual intercourse for money or it is a paid sex."

Prostitution is a worldwide social problem and it is said to be the oldest trade in the world. In India, prostitutes are especially looked down upon by society which has designated it to the lowest rungs of the social ladder as they do not seem to offer any meaningful contributions to the society. India has the largest market for prostitution in South Asia, with Mumbai alone being home to over 100,000 prostitutes. Every hour, four women or girls in India enter prostitution, three of them against their will. A large number of prostitutes in India are minors.

There are numerous reasons for increase in prostitution. Some of the common reasons are poverty, violence, profits, promotion of tourism in some countries, social customs (Devadasi system in ancient India), early marriage and desertion, ignorance and acceptance of prostitution. Generally, we think only women are the victims of prostitution but it is not like that even men and children are victims of it.

Sex workers are 10 times more at risk of HIV compared to the general population. As there are multiple sexual partners that predisposes sex workers for HIV infection. In 2023, 6.7 million people in Asia and the Pacific were living with HIV, making it the world's second largest epidemic after eastern and southern Africa. In 2023, 300,000 people in Asia and the Pacific were newly infected with HIV. This is a 14% decrease from 2010. In India, over 2.5 million people are living with HIV. The adult HIV prevalence is 0.2%, and annual new HIV infections are estimated at 66,400. This is a 44% reduction since 2010.

Measures to Tackle Prostitutions

Some of the solutions to eradicate prostitution are:

- Strict legal actions should be taken against those committing the crimes, such as forcing the children and girls for prostitution.
- Women empowerment and women education in the society.
- Vocational training to the girls and woman.
- Prosecution of women and child traffickers.

Rights of the Women

There is no law as such for prostitution but certainly the laws are there for the basic human rights of women and children which are equally reinforcing. The principle of gender equality is enshrined in the Indian Constitution in its Preamble, Fundamental Rights, Fundamental Duties and Directive Principles. The Constitution not only grants equality to women, but also empowers the state to adopt measures of positive discrimination in favor of women. Within the framework of a democratic polity, laws, development policies, plans and programs have aimed at women's advancement in different spheres of life. India has also ratified various international conventions and human rights instruments committing to secure equal rights of women. Key among them is the ratification of the Convention on Elimination of All Forms of Discrimination against Women (CEDAW) in 1993.

Special Initiatives for Women

- National Commission for Women
  - In January 1992, the Government set up this statutory body with a specific mandate to study and monitor all matters relating to the constitutional and legal safeguards provided for women,

review the existing legislation to suggest amendments wherever necessary, etc.
   - Reservation for women in local self-government.
   - The 73rd Constitutional Amendment Act passed in 1992 by Parliament ensure one-third of the total seats for women in all elected offices in local bodies whether in rural areas or urban areas.
- The National Plan of Action for the Girl Child (1991–2000)
   - The plan of action is to ensure survival, protection and development of the girl child with the ultimate objective of building up a better future for the girl child.
- National Policy for the Empowerment of Women, 2001.
   - The Department of Women and Child Development in the Ministry of Human Resource Development has prepared a "***National Policy for the Empowerment of Women***" in the year 2001. The goal of this policy is to bring about the advancement, development and empowerment of women.

Rights of the Children

Constitutional guarantees that are meant specifically for children include:
- Right to free and compulsory elementary education for all children in the 6–14 years, age group (Article 21A).
- Right to be protected from any hazardous employment till the age of 14 years (Article 24).
- Right to be protected from being abused and forced by economic necessity to enter occupations unsuited to their age or strength [Article 39(e)].
- Right to equal opportunities and facilities to develop in a healthy manner and in conditions of freedom and dignity and guaranteed protection of childhood and youth against exploitation and against moral and material abandonment [Article 39(f)].
- Right to early childhood care and education to all children until they complete the age of 6 years (Article 45).

CRIME

It is a great social problem faced by every society. It is relative, it is an act forbidden by law and there is penalty prescribed for it. Crime is the price paid for the civilization. It is a major problem in modern civilized societies. Although there is no limit to the crime list but some of the common crimes are:

- Robbery
- Murder
- Terrorism
- Cyber crimes
- Tax evading
- Assault or rape
- Corruption
- Black marketing

Our moral sense is at the lowest ebb. Terrorism has become the order of the day. The social causes of crime are disorganization, social competition, social mobility and conflict, defective social institutions, lack of education, sexual literacy, etc. Reform of the criminal is the main motive in his rehabilitation. In India, various measures are taken to give a better treatment in jails. Better food, clothing, recreational facilities, vocational training are given. The various handicrafts made by the prisoners are kept in exhibition also and the funds are further utilized for their welfare services.

DIVORCE

Initially marriage was considered as a bond which can never be broken as per Hinduism. But it is not only personal but also a legal issue. When there is problem in the relationship of husband and wife that cannot be settled on the grounds of mutual agreement or counseling, then the couple can proceed legally against it to get legal separation by law that is divorce. Divorce or legal termination of marriage is also known as dissolution of marriage. It is the process of cancelation or reorganizing of the legal duties and responsibilities of marriage, finally dissolving the bonds of matrimony between a married couple under the rule of the laws of that particular country or state.

Divorce laws vary around the world, but in most countries divorce requires the court sanction or other legal authority process, which may involve issues of alimony (spousal support), child custody, child visitation/access, parenting time, child support, distribution of property, and division of debt, etc.

DOWRY

A dowry is a transfer of either parental property, gifts or money at the marriage of a daughter sometimes demanded or it is by personal wish of the father also. Dowry is nothing but an extraction from bride's father. Dowry refers to money, gifts, goods or estate that wife brings to her husband's house because of marriage.

Dowry is a major problem of marriage in India, especially in certain areas. Nowadays, the amount of dowry is also increasing. Even the spread of modern education and enlightenment has not been able to diminish this problem.

DEFINITIONS

- "Dowry is the property which a woman brings with her or is given to her at the marriage." **—Encyclopedia: Britannica (Volume VII)**
- "The money, goods or estate which a woman brings to her husband in marriage." **—Webster's New World Dictionary**
- "The property which a man receives from his wife or her family at the time of marriage." **—Max Radin**

Causes

- **Endogamy:** Each caste and sub caste is endogamous and as such it restricts the area of male selections. Hence, in order to attract the groom and his family, dowry is demonstrated by the bride's side. The groom's family demands high amount of dowry as they know the scarcity of eligible grooms in community.
- **Child marriage:** In child marriage, the marrying partners are children. The rearing and other expenses are calculated by the families only.
- **Prestige symbol:** The giving and taking of dowry is a mutual act, and also the amount involved is very important for prestige of the families. Like "How much your son received in marriage? How much was given for your daughter's marriage" such questions are frequently answered just to sense proper prestige.
- **For marrying the girls who are not beautiful:** Father of the girl would like to have a good boy by offering huge sum of money as dowry for his not good looking daughter.
- **Customs:** The custom of "kanyadan" when the bride herself is gifted away, at that occasion usually she was given basic things to set up a small household for herself. But this custom has changed into compulsory dowry system.

Drawbacks or Demerits

- It is the root cause of the female feticide, because the birth of female child is the reason for the loan whereas the male child will help you to get money as dowry.
- As the girls cannot raise their voice against the marital issues so there is higher suicide rate among girls.
- The females are facing the psychological pressure and even the physical assault by the in-laws if they do not bring dowry with them.
- Just because parents do not want to pay dowry they had to marry their daughter to marry unsuitable persons like aged people, ugly men, evil characters, people of poor intellect, and unemployed persons.
- When a girl does not bring enough dowry, her status in the husband's family is poor. She is looked down upon.

Legal Actions

Dowry Prohibition Act, 1961

Since dowry is considered as a social evil, efforts had been made from time to time to eradicate it. Gandhiji was against dowry, and he educated the youth to be self-dependent, and take pledge not to have any dowry, various other efforts have also been made by teachers, voluntary workers, and young people themselves. Because of the increasing public opinion against dowry, dowry prohibition act was passed by the Central Government in 1961.

It may be worthwhile to give some consideration to the Dowry Prohibition Act, 1961. **The Dowry Prohibition Act, 1961**, defines it as "any property or valuable security which might be given or agreed to be given either directly or indirectly by one party to the other party in marriage, either by themselves or through parents or through any other person which may be present either before or at the time of marriage or even after that." The Act further states that any presents made at the time of marriage to either party in the form of cash, ornaments, clothes or other articles, unless they are made as considerations for the marriage of the said parties, shall not be deemed to be dowry.

Gifts given at the time of marriage are not included in dowry. This is a drawback. According to clause 5 any agreement regarding dowry is illegal. Any issue regarding dowry will be headed by a first class magistrate, according to clause 7. The complaint is to be made within one year of paying the dowry. The crime is not cognizable. Hence, its effect is relatively low. The law is often misused. Generally, none goes to the authorities to complain against the giving or taking of dowry.

Suggestions

- **Encourage intercaste and intercommunity marriages:** By following intercaste and intercommunity marriages, the difficulty of finding a mate within one's own caste/community is removed. When there is wide range of choice, and also freedom to choose, demands for dowry may come down.
- **Girls should be educated and economically independent:** If a girl is educated and employed, she is more confident and equipped to resist the demands for dowry. Such a girl may even refuse a man who demands dowry.
- **Encourage boys to stand on their own feet and then marry:** Generally, it is due to the economic dependence of the boys on their parents that they also become a part to the demand for dowry.
- **More effective legislation:** The present legislation cannot deliver the goods. Dowry should be made a cognizable crime and even gifts should be banned.
- **Equal rights to girls on father's property:** If girls are also given equal share of father's property (like that of the sons) the questions of dowry will not arise. This will further enhance the status of female child in the family and society.
- **Young people should pledge against taking or giving dowry:** If young men decide that they will not take dowry under any circumstances, and resist their parent's demands, this evil can be eradicated easily. Similarly, if young women decide not to marry those people who demand dowry, the problem can be solved.

JUVENILE DELINQUENCY

Juvenile delinquency is an antisocial behavior, crime or offense, committed by young people (male or female). Juvenile delinquent are simply under-age criminals that is, Juveniles who engage in offences that constitute crimes when committed by adults, and are between the age of

16 and 18 years, as prescribed by the law of the land. The maximum age today for juvenile delinquents according to the Juvenile Justice Act of 1986 is 16 years for boys and 18 years for girls.

DEFINITIONS

- Juvenile delinquency is "Any behavior which a given community at a given time considers in conflict with its best interest, whether or not the offender has been brought to court". —**Robinson**
- "Juvenile delinquency involves wrong doing by a child or young person who is under an age specified by the law of the place concerned". —**Sethna**

Thus, juvenile delinquency is any act of a child which is against the norms and values of a society, and which violates the law of the state.

Features

Following are some of the important features of juvenile delinquency in India:

- The delinquency rates are much higher among boys than among girls, that is, girls commit less delinquency than boys.
- The delinquency rates tend to be the highest during early adolescence (12–16 years, age group).
- Juvenile delinquency is more of an urban than a rural phenomenon.
- The metropolitan cities produce more juvenile delinquents than small cities and towns.
- Children living with parents and guardians are found to be more involved in the juvenile crimes.
- Low educational background is the prime attribute for delinquency.
- Poor economic background is another important characteristic of Juvenile delinquency in India.
- Though some delinquencies are committed in groups but the number of juvenile gangs having support of organized adult criminals is not much in our country.
- More than four-fifths of the juvenile delinquents are first offenders and only a little more than one-tenth are recidivists or past offenders.

Causes

There are several causes that are responsible for Juvenile delinquency. According to Healy and Bronner—"bad company, adolescent instability and impulses, early sex experiences, mental conflicts, extreme social stability, love for adventure, motion pictures, school dissatisfaction, poor recreation, street life, vocational dissatisfaction, sudden impulses and physical conditions of all sorts."

In India, some of the serious forms of juvenile delinquency are:

- Delinquent action against property such as stealing, damaging, etc.
- Murder and suicide
- Assault
- Gambling
- Sexual offences like rape and sodomy
- Ticket less travel especially in train
- Escape from custody
- Poverty
- Breakdown of joint family
- Breakdown of caste
- Breakdown of traditional religion, morals and values
- Illiteracy and lack of proper education
- Lack of care by the government
- Industrialization and urbanization, together with large scale migration to the cities
- Absence of proper facilities for marriage and family counseling, so as to have responsible and mature parenthood
- Political problems
- Social change

Control Remedy of Juvenile Delinquency

With regard to India, we may suggest the following measures to control and remedy the problem of juvenile delinquency.

- Proper assessment of the entire problem, in scientific and sociological manner.
- Improvement in economic condition
- Better education
- Training for parents to have responsible parenthood

- Revival in the system of religion and morals
- Facilities for proper treatment and reformation of Juvenile delinquents, with the provision of Juvenile courts and Juvenile police at the reformation centers.

DRUG ABUSE AND DRUG ADDICTION

"Drug abuse" is the use of illicit drug or misuse of legitimate drug resulting in the physical or psychological harm. It includes smoking *ganja* or hashish, taking heroin or cocaine or lysergic acid diethylamide (LSD), injecting morphine, drinking alcohol, and so forth. These are sometimes referred to as being high on "speed" or "trip" or "getting kicks".

The word "addiction" is generally used to describe physical dependence. Thus, "addiction" or "physical dependence" is a state whereby the body requires continued administration of the drug in order to function. Body functioning is interfered if the drug is withdrawn, and withdrawal symptoms appear in a pattern specific for the drug. The total reaction to deprivation is known as abstinence syndrome or withdrawal symptoms.

Signs of Drug Addiction

- An overpowering desires or need (compulsion) to continue taking the drug and to obtain it by any means.
- A tendency to increase the dose.
- A psychological and generally a physical dependence on the effects of the drugs.
- An effect detrimental to the individual and to the society.

Causes

There are several causes for drug abuse, some of which are the following:

- To get thrill or pleasure
- To relieve tension and to escape from situations of problem and anxiety
- Peer group pressure
- To satisfy curiosity
- To express independence or hostility
- Broken homes, family disorganization, and history of addiction in the family

- Age—the use of drugs usually starts either in adolescence or early youth
- Easy availability of drugs
- Urban life with its anonymity, wide circle of contacts and easy means of transportation encourage the use of drugs
- Strenuous work or studies
- Affluent mode of life

Drug abuse ruins one's life in several ways—health, career, prestige and, affect total life. Once the habit is established, it is very difficult to cure the problem. Hence, the quotation, "prevention is better than cure" is extremely important in respect of drug abuse.

Prevention of Drug Addiction

- **Primary prevention:** Primary prevention is through two main methods, (a) by limiting the availability of drugs, and (b) by educational measures. In all countries, there is legislation to control the production, supply, sale, possession and export of drugs. The underlying principle is that drugs should be made available for genuine medical use, but no surplus should be allowed in the market. These drugs should be guarded and controlled that none can be diverted for illicit use. The public, especially youth should be warned of the dangers of drug addiction and should be educated to use their time and energy in useful manners, e.g., drinking of alcohol is illegal at public places and same way some of the places such as schools, colleges and offices are declared as "No smoking zone".
- **Secondary prevention:** This is achieved through early identification of drug abusers that they can be treated promptly to prevent the development of complications. Any change in the behavior of young people should be closely watched. Remains of medicine, syringes and needles, pricks on the body, nervousness, restlessness and abnormal behavior of the young people should be watched closely. Get medical help as early as possible.
- **Tertiary prevention:** This is the treatment of the state of severe dependence. Many dedication centers, psychotherapists, social workers and social agencies are working to help the drug addicts. Help and support of family members is extremely important in overcoming the problem. Treatment of addicts is very important

not only for themselves but also for the society. Nowadays, there is additional danger of AIDS, because, this disease can spread through contaminated syringes and needles.

ALCOHOLISM

Alcoholism and drug addictions are detrimental not only to the health and welfare of the individual, but of the family, community and society and country at large. Alcoholism is condition in which an individual loses control over himself is constantly unable to refrain himself from drinking once he begins.

According to Keller and Efron, "alcoholism is characterized by repeated drinking of alcoholic beverages to an extent that it exceeds customary use or compliance with the social customs of the community and that adversely affect the drinker's health or interferes with his social or economic functioning."

Causes

- **Misery drinking:** Men often starts drinking in order to forget the miseries and problems of life. In the unending round of toil and dreariness, alcohol serves at least as a temporary escape.
- **Friendship:** Many people are drawn into this habit by friends. People start drinking just for company sake and many of them get addicted to it.
- **Fashion:** Drinking has become a fashion among many people, and it is taken as a sign of modernity and upper class.
- **Occupational factors:** Many men go for drinking because of physical exhaustion. Alcohol gives a temporary boost in energy and this helps them to do hard physical labor without the feeling of fatigue. Truck drivers, laborers, and other manual workers indulge in drinking due to this reason.
- **Ignorance:** Many of the hard physical laborers are under the impression that alcohol can give additional strength and vigor.
- **Weak personality:** A person whose moral fabric is weak and who gives way to temptations easily are led to drinking. Many weak people are not able to face the hard realities of life, and they find an easy escape in alcohol.

- **Unhealthy environment:** People living in slums or dilapidated conditions often find that they are surrounded by alcoholics. Soon they follow suit.
- **Sudden losses and frustration:** Sudden loss of a dear one, frustration in love, ruin of life's ambitions, and fall of business, all may lead people to drinking.
- **For business and professional reasons:** In modern world, people have to make new contracts to extend their business or to increase their professional contracts. Late night parties accompanied with alcohol have become a common feature.
- **The new elites:** Those people who become rich overnight have a tendency to take to drinks. They think it as an additional means to improve their social status.
- **Urbanization:** Modern city life with its mechanical ways of life, high materialistic values, and cut-throat competition all create tensions and conflict, and alcohol is accepted as a natural way of escape.
- **Social inadequacy:** Crisis in life may create a feeling of inadequacy and inferiority complex in the individual. There is a fundamental feeling of incompleteness. The victim of these crisis may take his first drink as an experimental method of dispelling the gloom which envelopes him.

Negative Effects of Drinking

- Drinking is a social evil and as far as possible every individual should keep himself away from it.
- Drinks affect the health of the people adversely.
- Alcoholics are more susceptible to many diseases especially that of liver.
- It leads to "crimes and lawlessness".
- Addiction, if it occurs among students, adversely affects not only their studies but also affects the career.
- Alcoholism is a root cause of family unhappiness, problems, tensions and even total disorganization, as a man spends his whole earning on alcohol, his family is left to starve.
- Drinking is often associated with other social evils like gambling, prostitution and other vices.

Suggestions for Control and Eradication

- **The working condition:** Alcoholism is generally found more among the industrial workers, agricultural laborers and also those who are employed in strenuous manual occupations. This problem is more in India. If the problem is to be eradicated the working conditions are to be improved.
- **Mass education:** Mass education about the evils of drinking through various means of communication. Public lectures, film shows, songs, dramas, radios, televisions, all methods should be adopted to convince the people.
- **Recreation:** Recreational facilities should be provided. Healthy recreation will divert the minds of people and keep them away from the habit of drinking.
- **Housing facilities:** Housing facilities are provided for the workers, either by the management or by the government, so that the workers can bring their families to the cities where they work.
- **Antidrinking movements:** Women should undertake anti-drinking movements, because women are the worst sufferers if the men-folk drink and behave irresponsibly.
- **Brothels:** Brothels should be away from the residence of industrial workers. It is said that wine and women usually go together.

HANDICAPPED OR DISABILITY

- In India. 4.52% population is disabled according to latest reports (NFHS-5 survey (2019–21). Locomotor disabilities accounted for 44.70% of all disabilities, followed by mental and speech disabilities.
- The children with physical and mental disabilities experience personal limitations in the physical, social, psychological and economic spheres, some of which can be alleviated with parental, community and governmental support.
- The aim is developing and maintaining a focus on abilities rather than on disabilities. This is the reason why handicapped persons are now called physically challenged so as to leave a positive carry over impact on the person as well as the family.
- Many children face social discrimination unlike the caste and class system. Disabled children stand out as different, and may become

soft targets for exploitation, bullying and mockery. They should know that they do not deserve victimization and isolation. Sports can provide an effective way to strengthen socialization. When paired with developmentally similar peers and supportive adult guidance, children learn about teamwork, cooperation and fair play. They are even proved to be even more efficient than a normal individual sometimes, where they become the role models to the society.

POPULATION

"A population is wholesome of all the organisms of the same group or species, which live in a particular geographical area, and have the capability of reproduction."

Population explosion is also known as over population. The birth rate, death rate, fertility rate are some of the indicators of the population increase. As the population increases there is scarcity of the resources and increase in social problems also. The population explosion is the root cause of majority of the social problems. When the population increases, there is poor social control.

Common social problems due to population explosion are:
- Pollution
- Unemployment
- Poverty
- Increased crime rates such as robbery, beggary and murder
- Prostitution
- Child labor
- Less land for cultivation, low production rate
- Increased economic burden

SLUMS

Slums are densely populated urban informal settlements of families which are characterized by substandard housing.

Characteristics of slums are:
- **Location:** Most of the slums occupy the outskirts of the city or towns.
- **Population:** The slums possess very dense population, and the rate of population growth is very high.
- **Housing:** There is variety of the housing infrastructure, from huts till professionally built house.

- **Sanitation:** Poor hygienic conditions are seen in most of the slums.
- **Water supply:** There is always issue of water supply and electricity and other problems also.

Example of slums in India is "Dharavi" which is a locality in Mumbai, Maharashtra. This slum is one of the largest slums in the world; it is a home to roughly 700,000 to about 1 million people, and Dharavi is the second-largest slum in the continent of Asia and the third-largest slum in the world.

Social problems due to slums:

- More of communicable diseases due to poor hygienic conditions and dense population.
- Higher crime rate
- Violence
- Poverty
- Prostitution
- Child labor
- Robbery
- Illiteracy

SOCIAL AGENCIES AND REMEDIAL MEASURES

There are three common agencies in the society which look after social problems. These are:

Informal Agencies

These are society controls, social behavior, and social relationships. This is done through various agencies like family, religion and law.

Family

- Home is the first institution and the family is the teacher for every child.
- Family is the ancient and effective agency of the social control.
- Extended and joint families were good to teach moral values and social behavior as compared to nuclear families.
- Nowadays the nuclear families are very common where there is mother, father and the children in the family. Most of the parents are busy either with their job or the household work and there is very less time for teaching the social norms to the child.

- Divorce rates are drastically increasing in the society making the children to stay with single parent in a family.
- If family educates the moral values, unity, being in group, sharing and adjusting to its children then there will be less social problems such as anger related problems, crimes and broken families, divorce, dowry, etc.

Religion

- In ancient times, when there were no means of social control and the problems were arising day by day then the concept of supernatural power came into existence, and basically "it is the belief in the supernatural powers."
- Religion never promotes the violence and disharmony in the society.
- The sole aim of every religion is to direct mankind for a peaceful society and prosperous environment.
- But many times there are violence and chaos on the basis of religion, India being a country with multiple religion, is more vulnerable to the religion-based violence and riots.
- The holy books like 'Ramayan' and 'Quran' always guide the human toward the love and unity.

Formal Agencies

Law

- The law is the ultimate power that governs the small and large institutions and country smoothly.
- When there is a law, there is provision of punishment if the rules are violated which enforces a higher standard of the law to be implemented in general population.
- The various social issues which are very difficult to solve otherwise can be easily managed through the legal support.
- The different acts and laws are meant for the effective social control.

Other Agencies

Various agencies such as:

- School, colleges, hospitals, nongovernmental and governmental organizations identify and work for the different social problems. The curriculum in education from basic education till advanced education is designed in such a way that it not only highlights each and every social issue but also makes an individual capable of solving the problems.

- Each and every profession is designed in such a way that it is for the social welfare only, be it medical profession, defence or teaching profession all are directed to social service only.

SUMMARY

- Social problems are the behavior pattern or situations that are considered objectionable or undesirable in society.
- Prostitution is a worldwide social problem and it is said to be the oldest trade in the world.
- Some of the common reasons of prostitution are poverty, violence, profits, promotion of tourism in some countries, social customs, early marriage and desertion, ignorance and acceptance of prostitution.
- There is no law as such for prostitution but certainly the laws are there for the basic human rights of women and children which are equally reinforcing.
- Crime is the price paid for the civilization.
- The social causes of crime are disorganization, social competition, social mobility and conflict, defective social institutions, lack of education, sexual literacy, etc.
- Divorce laws vary around the world, but in most countries, divorce requires the court sanction or other legal authority process.
- Dowry refers to money, gifts, goods or estate that wife brings to her husband's house because of marriage.
- Juvenile delinquency is an antisocial behavior, crime or offense, committed by young people (male or female).
- Drug abuse is the use of illicit drug or misuse of legitimate drug resulting in the physical or psychological harm.
- Drug abuse ruins one's life in several ways—health, career, prestige and also affect total life.
- Treatment of addicts is very important not only for themselves but also for the society.
- Alcoholism is condition in which an individual loses control over himself and is constantly unable to refrain himself from drinking once he begins.
- Disabled children stand out as different, and may become soft targets for exploitation, bullying and mockery.
- The birth rate, death rate, fertility rate are some of the indicators of the population increase.
- Slums are densely populated urban informal settlements of families which are characterized by substandard housing.
- Each and every profession is designed in such a way that it is for the social welfare only.

STUDENT ASSIGNMENT

LONG ANSWER QUESTIONS

1. Enlist various social problems in India and explain any one in detail.
2. Explain causes of dowry and the suggestions to control dowry.

SHORT ANSWER QUESTIONS

1. Define the following:
    a. Dowry
    b. Juvenile delinquency
2. Identify the root causes of poverty in contemporary societies. How do these factors contribute to perpetuating cycles of poverty?
3. How does climate change exacerbate social inequalities and pose challenges for vulnerable populations such as low-income communities and marginalized groups? Provide specific examples.
4. Explain the social problems associated with rapid urbanization.
5. What are some key challenges faced by cities in terms of housing, transportation, and social services?

MULTIPLE CHOICE QUESTIONS

1. **Which of the following is not a characteristic of social problem?**
    a. Generally regarded harmful for the society
    b. It has effect on a large section of a society
    c. Develops gradually and slowly
    d. All of the above
2. **Which of the following is not a source of social problem?**
    a. Social change
    b. Poverty
    c. Personal development
    d. Personal disorganization

3. **Density of population is very much related to:**

a. Climate | b. Political system
c. Environmental study | d. Economic condition

4. **Which is an institution to rehabilitate juvenile delinquents?**

a. Juvenile Courts | b. Remand Homes
c. Foster Homes | d. All of these

5. **Which is the cause of rapid growth of population in India?**

a. Peaceful conditions
b. Excess birth over death
c. Progress in medical facilities
d. All of the above

6. **What is the effect of overpopulation?**

a. Population and poverty | b. Low per capita income
c. Shortage of food | d. All of these

7. **Poverty is a:**

a. Social problem | b. Economic problem
c. Political problem | d. Religious problem

ANSWER KEY

1. c **2.** c **3.** a **4.** d **5.** d **6.** d **7.** a

Notes

10

Community

LEARNING OBJECTIVES

After the completion of the chapter, the readers will be able to:

- Define community.
- Explain the types of community.
- Describe about community development project.
- Discuss healthcare delivery system in India.

CHAPTER OUTLINE

- Meaning
- Types of Community
- Community Development Project
- Important Programs of Community Development and Integrated Rural Development

KEY TERMS

City: A densely-populated urban area characterized by a high concentration of people, diverse economic activities, and advanced infrastructure and services.
Community: A group who follows a social structure within a society.
Population growth: The increase in the number of individuals within a population over time, influenced by factors such as birth rates, death rates, immigration, and emigration.
Rural community: A community located in non-urban areas characterized by lower population density, agricultural activities, and often close-knit social relationships.
Tribal community: A community consisting of indigenous or native populations, often characterized by shared cultural practices, traditions, and governance systems rooted in ancestral heritage.
Urbanization: The process of increasing population concentration in urban areas due to rural-to-urban migration and natural population growth, leading to significant socioeconomic and environmental changes.

A community is a group of people. An individual forms the family, which is the smallest functional unit of the society. Community is small or may be large social group where they share the common religion, norms, beliefs and values. Community has well-defined geographical boundaries and is relatively permanent. Each and every community is socially recognized by a name. The community has no legal status.

MEANING

"An area of social living marked by some degree of social coherence."

DEFINITIONS

- "Community is a social group with some degree of 'we feeling' and living in a given area." **—Bogardus**
- "Community is the smallest territorial group that can embrace all aspects of social life." **—Kingsley Davis**

TYPES OF COMMUNITY

Rural Community

Rural means "belonging to the country." The word village is derived from the Latin word **villaticus** means 'belonging to a farmhouse'. There is a sense of **we feeling** and cooperation. Agriculture is said to be the starting point of human civilization as it helped man to have a settled life in a village and village and the farmers are the one who produce the cereals. According to 2021 census, the village population in India was about 68.8% of the total population. An overwhelming majority of India's population live in >6 lakh 40 thousand 9 hundred and 30 villages.

DEFINITIONS

- "The rural community comprises the constellation of institutions and persons grouped about a small center and sharing common primary interest." **—Eldredge and Merrill**
- "The village is unit of rural society. It is the theater where in the quantum of rural life unfolds itself and functions." **—A R Desai**

Characteristics

- **Occupation:** The main occupation of the people in rural community is agriculture, animal husbandry, poultry and apiculture and fishing, beekeeping, etc.
- **Dressing:** Most of the villages follow the traditional pattern of dressing.
- **Environment:** Villages have natural surroundings. Animals, birds, river, ponds and all other natural things are common in the village. There is a saying that village is made by God or nature.
- **Social stratification:** The caste system and class system is very much prevalent among the village population due to their deeply rooted beliefs and customs.
- **Size:** The village communities are small in size. There may be a few households or small number of people.
- **Population:** As the villages have large areas of land for cultivation the number of inhabitants is small. However, in our Indian villages the particular habitat is overcrowded, while the land around is spacious. Therefore, if one considers the density of the real habitat of the village—it is high, many families live huddled up, in fact there is no road even to have convenient transportation.
- **Mode of communication:** The minimum use of the electronics and technology is seen in the villages.
- **Homogeneity:** The village life has much homogeneity. People of a village have common occupation and common way of living.
- **Mobility:** Mobility means movement or migration of people from one place to another or from one social status to another, i.e., there are two types of mobilities, physical as well as social. Both are limited in villages, especially in Indian villages.
- **Social relations:** The rural communities are small and have good relationships among themselves and better social awareness also. The village is like a large family. Everyone is known personally.
- **Type of families in village:** Village usually has larger families or extended or there may be joint families too.
- **Education:** Earlier most of the villagers were engaged in agriculture, but nowadays advanced education and specialization are also common in villages.

- **Political awareness:** Political consciousness, participations and awareness are less in villages.
- **Social problems:** Social problems such as crime rate, juvenile delinquency, prostitution and murder are less in villages. But Indian villages have different social problems like ignorance, superstition, poverty, unemployment and conflicts based on caste system are profound.
- **Public opinion:** Public opinion is not easily changeable in villages due to the rigidity of customs, traditions and values. Education, transportation, communication, and new ideas can help in changing the public opinion in villages too.
- **Child marriages:** Child marriage is still there in Indian villages. Lack of education, cultural practices and social values promote child marriages.
- **Women status in society:** Women are not considered to be very significant part of the society, especially to take decisions for themselves and also in family matters. There is still male dominance. The rate of literacy and education is also relatively less among women.

Changes in Rural Community

Change is a natural phenomenon. Nothing is static in the society. But in traditional societies change is sometimes slow and it may not be even significant. Rural India is witnessing changes from ancient time.

Factors Affecting Changes in Rural Community

There are certain major factors which encourage changes in rural India, as shown below:

- **Natural calamities such as floods, famines and earthquakes:** These phenomena have really uprooted the rural people from time to time. Despite of destructions of life and property, there is social mobility also. When people shift from their original habitat a lot of changes do take place which is natural.
- **Population growth:** Population explosion really takes place in rural India. Due to illiteracy, ignorance and absence of social enlightenment the births are not controlled, and even the use of contraception is less. It may be due to personal and social factors like the density of

population on the land, people migrating to urban areas in search of livelihood and better facilities and career opportunities.

- **Industrialization and urbanization:** Industrial revolution and the vicious process of industrialization and urbanization have greatly affected the socioeconomic life of man. It is not only affecting changes in occupations or lifestyle but the complete patterns of living are affected.
- **Education:** Education is primary and only tool to bring the change. Education extends one's outlook and perception to changes. Many schools and colleges are made and the promotion of education is done at larger scale. The educated people from villages are migrating to cities for higher education and employment. Along with educated children their families also migrate to urban areas. Thus, education is responsible for significant changes in rural India.
- **Sanitation and hygiene:** As the open field defecation is very common in villages and that is not the only cause of pollution but also a very common source of diseases such as Polio and hepatitis. At present, the need of Swachh Bharat is highlighted and specifically in villages the construction of toilets is made compulsory in each and every home and the government is also funding for this.
- **Transportation:** The transportation facilities are now greatly upgraded to villages also. The connectivity through train is also promoted, highways and construction of the airports is also done at so many villages round the country. For example, the connectivity through metro train has connected number of villages to extend the convenience to rural population for higher education and occupation.
- **Communication:** The communication facilities are being extended to rural areas. With the advent of radio, even the illiterate masses could hear information and learn it. Nowadays the internet is also very common in village population due to the cost effective and easy accessibility of the internet facility with smartphones. The government has extended television facilities to most of the rural areas and this is going to be a powerful agent of social change.
- **Political leadership:** The effects of political parties and political leadership can be easily observed in villages nowadays. Even the election of the village panchayat is influenced by political parties and their leaders.

- **Government efforts:** The Central and State Government have several new and old programs, which are useful to bring changes in rural life. The programs such as twenty-point program, national health mission, etc. from the government aimed at the rural change in many ways. Community development projects and the program of the village **panchayat** also make changes in villages.
- **Social problems:** There are different social problems that are prevalent in rural population as compared to urban India due to different lifestyle and geographical differences. Poverty, illiteracy, unemployment, female feticide, social discrimination on the basis of caste and untouchability, and many other problems are prevalent among the villagers that necessitate them to change their traditional mode of living.
- **Changes in villages:** Many changes are currently taking place in villages such as lifestyle, health habits, social awareness, street lights and water supply, etc.
- **Change in rural marriage and family:** Child marriage has been very common social problem since ancient times. It is still prevalent. There are boys and girls who are educated or who get married soon after attaining adulthood. Thus, there is change in child marriage up to some extent.
  - The joint families and extended families are changing into smaller or nuclear families.
  - The authority of the father as the head of the family is also undergoing some changes especially in families where the mother and children are educated.
  - The status of women in family has also changed especially where the members of the family are educated.
- **Economic status:** Nowadays villagers are adopting the scientific agriculture. Some have already started mechanical farming. Hybrid seeds and manures are also used.
  - Caste based traditional occupations are also undergoing changes, although there are people who still pursue the traditional jobs.
  - The people in villages have improved their standards of living.
  - The housing, the style of dressing, the types of food consumed, and the types of utensils used in the house are also changing.

- **Changes in social life:**
  - The hold of caste and untouchability is on the decline. It will, however, take much time to wipe out the practices of caste system and social discrimination from Indian villages.
  - Scheduled castes and tribes are receiving help from the government in order to improve their socioeconomic conditions.

Urban Community

There were cities in ancient times also, but most of them were important due to one or the other reason as religion, politics, trade or commerce. But the modern cities are mostly of great industrial importance because of which people come to cities from villages and this is also the reason for the growth and development of modern cities.

Growth of Cities

While cities have existed since ancient times, but recently they represent only a small proportion of the total population. The lives of the majority of the people were shaped by the rural community or villages only. The massive growth of metropolitan cities has been a characteristic feature since past six decades or so.

Although the growth of cities greatly depends on birth and death rates and migration but political, religious, historical and economic factors equally contribute. The urban development has specific centers which serve as power places for a particular area. For example:

- Political centers can be the capital of states (Bhopal, Jaipur, Mumbai, Kolkata) or the center of political activities (Delhi).
- Training centers for the military (Kharagvasla) or centers for defense (Jodhpur).
- Economic centers are areas which predominate in trade or commerce (e.g., Ahmedabad, Surat) and industrial towns are places with factories.
- The religious cities are those where people go on pilgrimage (Haridwar, Varanasi, Allahabad).
- Educational centers have educational institutions (Pilani).

Differences between urban and rural societies are enlisted in Table 10.1.

TABLE 10.1: Differences between urban and rural societies

Dimension	Urban societies	Rural societies
Economy	Dominated by secondary and tertiary activities	Predominantly primary industry and activities supporting it
Occupational structure	Manufacturing, construction, administration and service activities	Agriculture and other primary industry occupations
Education levels and provision	Higher than national averages	Lower than national averages
Accessibility to services	High	Low
Accessibility to information	High	Low
Demography	Low fertility and mortality	High fertility and mortality
Politics	Greater representation of liberal and radical elements	Conservative, resistance to change
Ethnicity	Varied	More homogeneous
Migration levels	High and generally net immigration	Low and generally net out emigration

DEFINITIONS

Definitions of city

- "A city is a limited geographical area inhabited by a large and closely settled population having many common interests and institutions under a local government authorized by the state". **—Howard Woolston**
- "City is a state of mind, a body of customs and traditions and the organized attitudes and sentiments that are inherent in these customs". **—Robert Park**

Thus, it can be concluded that city or the urban community has a limited area, a local government and some traits which makes the city entirely different from the rural community.

Characteristics of City

- **Occupation:** The urban people are engaged in different variety of occupations such as medical, trade, commerce, education, government and recreation. There are numerous occupation options available in the urban community areas.
- **Environment:** The environment is quite artificial. The factories, shops, malls, railways, buildings and many other things are all created by man. There is not much naturalism in air and environment both.
- **Size:** Cities are the larger communities as compared to rural area, and their population may be in lakhs, millions or crores. This is because in a small land area, very large number of people reside.
- **Population:** The density of population is really very high. There is overcrowding and congestion. Slums are also created. Due to such situations the health status of the urban populations is also not satisfactory despite of good healthcare services.
- **Urban life:** There are no similarities in the life of the urban people. There is diversity in the fields of occupation, language, religion and the culture because people from different places are residing in an urban community.
- **Social stratification:** The people in urban community are stratified on the basis of the class and economic status, the caste system is least prevalent here. The lifestyle of the people also varies according to religion, occupations and other socioeconomic status.
- **Social mobility:** In city, mobility is very easy and quick. The urban man can rise or lower his status to a greater extent during his lifetime and the competition for status is very common here. The exercise of talent, the achievement of education, and display of wealth are common in urban community.
- **Communication:** The mode of communication is electronic media to a larger extent but some of the official information is also communicated by post, newspaper and magazines too.
- **Family:** The urban families are smaller in size than the rural families. Family mostly includes husband, wife and children. Large family is not that common in the city.
- **Social problems:** The urban community has different social problems such as higher crime rates, juvenile delinquency, rape, assault, murder, theft, kidnapping, prostitution, divorce and family disorganizations. They are very common in cities all over the world.

Social Problems in Urban Community

Urban problems have no limits, everyday new problems are identified such as—pollution, crime, juvenile delinquency, begging, alcoholism, corruption, and unemployment. Apart from these:

- Substance abuse
- Elderly abuse
- Rape and assault
- Broken families
- Housing and slums
- Crowding and depersonalization
- Water supply and drainage
- Waste disposal
- Transportation and traffic
- Power shortage
- Pollution

Causes of Urban Problems

The causes of urban problems in India are as follows:

- **Social mobility:** People migrate to cities for better employment, opportunities or education.
- **Industrialization:** The urban population growth rate is 4% in India the industrial growth rate is about 6% per year. The Eighth Five Year Plan postulated an industrial growth rate of 8% per annum. This growth was expected to take care of the additional job requirements in the cities.
- **Government initiatives:** Municipal corporations look after the needs which are further divided into zones and there is always transfer of responsibilities from state to central government. The governments have not kept pace with city growth either spatially or in terms of management infrastructure. There is neither the will nor the capacity to plan for the future.
- **Poor planning:** Nowadays each and every profession is merely a way of earning but the professional efforts are not that evident, as in case of civil services and administration services the authorized person should have a vision and mission, which is greatly missing.

- **Population:** By the day some proper plans for the social problems come up, there is a great increase in urban population, which again multiplies the problems in the society.

Differences between rural and urban communities are enlisted in Table 10.2.

TABLE 10.2: Differences between rural and urban community

Rural community	Urban community
The rural society is homogeneous	The urban society is heterogeneous
Rural community is dominated by primary relations	Urban community is dominated by secondary relations
The people are simple, hospitable, and generous	People are artificial, and self-centered
Informal means of social control are enough to regulate interpersonal relations	Formal means of social control like law, legislation and police, etc., are necessary in addition to the informal means to regulate the behavior of people
Rural society is less mobile	Urban society is more mobile
The people in rural society are more conservative, orthodox and dogmatic	The people in urban areas are more competitive and progressive
The women in rural community are traditional housewives and mostly have basic education only	The women are employed, well-educated and are career conscious
The people follow caste system of social stratification	The caste system is not common but class system is very common
The environment is natural and less polluted	The environment is highly polluted and not natural
The families are mostly extended or joint families	The families are mostly nuclear families
The population is not densely packed in terms of housing	The population is very densely packed in terms of housing
The common occupation of rural community is agriculture and allied occupations such as cattle breeding, poultry and handicrafts	Most of the occupations are nonagricultural occupations such as industry trade, commerce, teaching, nursing, medical and administration, etc.

Contd...

Rural community	Urban community
The size of community is small within the count of hundreds or thousands	The size of community is large with the count of lakhs or millions
There is a common language and culture in a village	The language and culture greatly differ as the people from different places are living together
Education status is not that good	Education status is comparatively good

COMMUNITY DEVELOPMENT PROJECT

The development of community is the basic need of the era that demands a change in the mental outlook of the people, an urge to reach higher standard of life is a strong will to achieve it. The community development projects aim at a comprehensive and all round development of rural population.

The Planning Commission—Government of India has defined community development as "an attempt to bring about a social and economic transformation of village life through the efforts of the people themselves."

Aims and Objectives of Community Development Project

- Integrated development of rural community covering, social, cultural and economic aspects of rural life.
- Fullest development of available material and human resources.
- Development of a sense of responsibility and awareness among the villagers.
- Development of initiative among the villagers.
- Development of agriculture and allied matters like animal husbandry.
- Development of social life by providing better communication.
- Development of cottage industries.
- Providing more opportunities for employment.
- Development of cooperative effort at rural level.
- Women and child welfare.

Community Development Program

The Community Development Program was launched in 55 selected projects on October 2, 1952 each project covering an area of 30 villages with a population of about 3 lakhs. The pattern was revised in 1958. According to the new pattern, a block covered an area of 400–500 square km. In hundred villages, a population of 60–70 thousand resides. The block has two active stages of operation. First stage of 5 years, followed by the second stage again of 5 years. Then the block enters the past development phase. A functional assistance of '2 lakhs' for first stage and '5 lakhs' for the second stage is provided.

Stages in Organization of Community Development Programs (Fig. 10.1)

- **At the central level:** Community development is under the Ministry of Agriculture and Irrigation.
- **At the state level:** There is a development community with the chief minister as its chairman and ministers are the members of different departments.
- **At the district level:** There is a district board for developmental work. This board is constituted by selected representatives like the Members of Parliament, Members of Legislature Assemblies and heads block level panchayats. In every district, there is a village level, planning committees also with the district collector as its chief.
- **At the block level there are block panchayats,** which look after developmental work. One block development officer and eight extension officers for agriculture, cooperation, animal husbandry, panchayat, court age, industry, social education and women and child welfare are appointed at the block level.

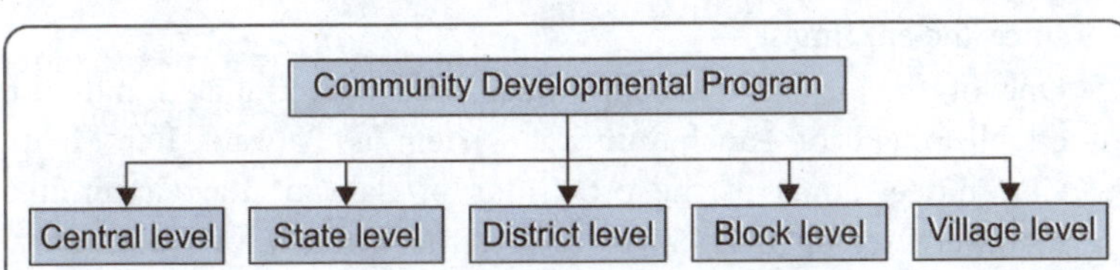

FIGURE 10.1: Stages in organization of community development programs

- **Village level panchayats** are responsible for looking after village level work. Our village level worker is appointed for a group of ten villages. Extension workers also help in the village level work. In addition to the women, village level workers are also appointed.

IMPORTANT PROGRAMS OF COMMUNITY DEVELOPMENT AND INTEGRATED RURAL DEVELOPMENT

Panchayati Raj System and Social Dynamics

- A democratic system is one of the prominent forms of government that is practiced in almost all the countries in the modern world. India being the largest democracy in the world has been a pioneer in effectively practicing democratic principles in its true sense. This has been proven in the introduction of practice of decentralized form of government through Panchayati Raj System. The Government of India enacted in the 73rd Constitution Amendment Act, which was passed by Parliament in 1992 and with effect from April 24, 1993 after the required number of State Legislatures ratified the same.
- Panchayati Raj is a three-tier structure of democratic institutions at district, block and village levels namely, Zila Parishad, Panchayat Samiti and Village Panchayats respectively. It is a system of local self-government aimed at securing gram swaraj. It is based on the philosophy of decentralization; further enables participative governance by the people. It is a suitable institutional arrangement for achieving rural development through people's initiative.
- Panchayats as local self-government institutions and vehicles of development have been parts of the Indian system of governance since ancient times.
- One of the prominent committees that were initiated into the establishment of Panchayati Raj System is Balwant Rai Mehta Committee. Some of the provisions of Balwant Rai Committee that were set up in 1957 to review the working of Community Development program were:
  - The introduction of a three-tier system of panchayats in the process of democratic decentralization and village reconstruction was a pivotal suggestion made by the committee.

- The committee felt that democratic government composed, controlled and directed by popular representation of the local areas is necessary at the local level.
- The report strongly recommended that training requirements of panchayat personnel should be given high priority.
- It was Gandhiji's idea that India lives in its villages. In this pretext, the government felt that local governance would lead to achieving Gandhiji's dream and hence Panchayati Raj System has been moving in that path. Its main objective is that rural people should undertake the responsibilities of governing themselves, and their active participation in the developmental activities in agriculture, animal husbandry, irrigation, public health and education.
- Panchayat has made a huge impact on social mobilization and participation of the rural people for the sake of their development. Panchayati Raj System has provided avenues for facilitating people's participation at the grass root level in the following ways:
  - Gram Sabha has provided an open forum for discussion at various village level development activities thereby ensuring people's participation effectively in the political and social system.
  - Representation of weaker sections in the decision-making process has paved way for these sections to uplift themselves and others who are equally deprived of their opportunities.
  - Empowering rural women through an induction of 1/3 reservation in the Panchayati Raj bodies has been a positive improvement because in the era of equality, women also need to have economic, political and social equality along with men.
  - Panchayat Raj System has been an edifice in the functioning of democracy in India. As per the Constitution, panchayats in their respective areas would prepare plans for economic development and social justice and also execute them. To facilitate this, as per State Finance Commission's recommended states are supposed to devolve functions to panchayats and also make funds available for doing these. The functions of panchayats are divided among different committees which are called Standing Committees/Sthayee

Samitis/Upa Samitis, etc. One of the members remains in charge of each of such committees while the overall charge rests with the chairperson of the panchayat. Panchayats are supported by a host of other officials, the number of which varies from state to state.

- Apart from grants received from the government under the recommendation of the Finance Commission, panchayats receive schematic funds for implementation of schemes (Mahatma Gandhi National Rural Employment Guarantee Act (MGNREGA), Backward Regions Grant Fund (BRGF), Indira Awaas Yojana (IAY), etc. They can also raise revenue by imposing taxes, fees, penalties, etc., as per rule of the state.
- Seventy-third constitution amendment of the constitution gives important powers and responsibilities to Panchayati Raj Systems in development and progress of rural society. As rural society is mainly concentrated in rural areas, the major functions of Panchayati Raj system are as following:
  - Agricultural development and irrigation facilities
  - Land reforms
  - Eradication of poverty
  - Dairy farming, poultry, piggery and fish rearing
  - Rural housing
  - Provision of safe drinking water
  - Social forestry, fodder and fuel
  - Providing primary education, adult education and informal training
  - Constructions of roads, buildings, schools and hospitals
  - Maintenance and regulation of markets and fairs
  - Preference to child and women development
  - Look into the welfare of weaker sections, scheduled castes, scheduled tribes and other deprived sections of the society.

Healthcare Delivery System in India

India is a country of 28 states and 8 union territories. States are largely independent in matters related to the delivery of healthcare to the people. Each state has developed its own system of healthcare delivery, independent of the Central Government (Fig. 10.2). The Central

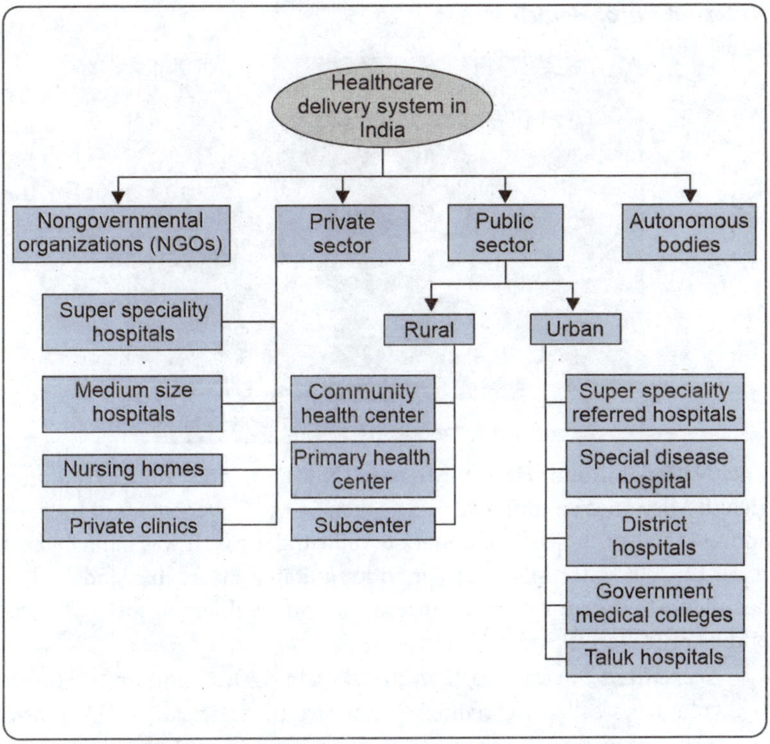

FIGURE 10.2: Healthcare delivery system in India

Government's responsibility mainly consists of policy making, planning, guiding, assisting, evaluating and coordinating the work of the State Health Ministries. The health system in India has three main links:

1. Central
2. State
3. Local or peripheral

Rural Healthcare Services

The healthcare services in rural areas are different considering the different health problems of rural population. Grossly rural health problems came in limelight from 2005 with the National Rural Health Mission, which covers all the rural population of India.

National Rural Health Mission, 2005

The National Rural Health Mission (NRHM), now under National Health Mission is an initiative undertaken by the Government of India to address the health needs of under-served rural areas. It was launched on April 12, 2005. NRHM seeks to provide equitable, affordable, and quality healthcare to the rural population, especially the vulnerable groups. Some of the key initiatives in NRHM include:

- **Accredited Social Health Activists (ASHA):** Community Health volunteers called Accredited Social Health Activists (ASHAs) have been engaged under the mission for establishing a link between the community and the health system.
- **Rogi Kalyan Samiti (Patient Welfare Committee)/Hospital Management Society**: It is a management structure that acts as a group of trustees for the hospitals to manage the affairs of the hospital. Financial assistance is provided to these Committees through untied fund to undertake activities for patient welfare.
- **Untied Grants to Subcenters:** Untied Grants to Subcenters have been used to fund grass-root improvements in healthcare. Some examples include:
    - Improved efficacy of Auxiliary Nurse Midwives (ANMs) in the field that can undertake better antenatal care and other healthcare services.
    - Village Health Sanitation and Nutrition Committees (VHSNC) have used untied grants to increase involvement in their local communities to address the needs of poor households and children.

- **Healthcare contractors**: NRHM has provided healthcare contractors to underserved areas, and has been involved in training to expand the skill set of doctors at strategically located facilities identified by the states.
- **Janani Suraksha Yojana (JSY):** JSY aims to reduce maternal mortality among pregnant women by encouraging them to deliver in government health facilities. Under the scheme, cash assistance is provided to eligible pregnant women for giving birth in a government health facility. Large scale demand side financing under the JSY has brought poor households to public sector health facilities on a scale never witnessed before.
- **National Mobile Medical Units (NMMUs):** Many underserved areas have been covered through National Mobile Medical Units (NMMUs).
- **National Ambulance Services:** Free ambulance services are provided in every nook and corner of the country connected with a toll free number and reaches within 30 minutes of the call.
- **Janani Shishu Suraksha Karyakram (JSSK):** As part of recent initiatives and further moving in the direction of universal healthcare, Janani Shishu Suraksha Karyakarm (JSSK) was introduced to provide free to and fro transport, free drugs, free diagnostic, free blood, and free diet to pregnant women who come for delivery in public health institutions and sick infants up to one year.
- **Rashtriya Bal Swasthya Karyakram (RBSK):** The Child Health Screening and Early Intervention Services have been launched in February 2013 to screen diseases specific to childhood, developmental delays, disabilities, birth defects and deficiencies. The initiative covers about 27 crore children between 0 and 18 years of age and also provides free treatment including surgery for health problems diagnosed under this initiative.
- **Mother and Child Health Wings (MCH Wings):** With a focus to reduce maternal and child mortality, dedicated Mother and Child Health Wings with 100/50/30 bed capacity have been sanctioned in high case load district hospitals and CHCs which would create additional beds for mothers and children.
- **Free Drugs and Free Diagnostic Service:** A new initiative is launched under the National Health Mission to provide Free Drugs

Service and Free Diagnostic Service with a motive to lower the out of pocket expenditure on health.

District Hospital and Knowledge Center (DHKC)

As a new initiative, District Hospitals are being strengthened to provide Multispecialty healthcare including dialysis care, intensive cardiac care, cancer treatment, mental illness, emergency medical and trauma care, etc. These hospitals would act as the knowledge support for clinical care in facilities below it through a telemedicine center located in the district headquarters and also developed as centers for training of paramedics and nurses.

National Iron+ Initiative

The National Iron+ Initiative is an attempt to look at Iron Deficiency Anemia in which beneficiaries will receive iron and folic acid supplementation irrespective of their Iron/Hb status. This initiative will bring together existing programs (IFA supplementation for: pregnant and lactating women and; children in the age group of 6–60 months) and introduce new age groups.

Urban Healthcare Services

National Urban Health Mission

The National Urban Health Mission (NUHM) as a sub-mission of National Health Mission (NHM) has been approved by the Cabinet on May 1, 2013. NUHM envisages to meet healthcare needs of the urban population with the focus on urban poor, by making available to them essential primary healthcare services and reducing their out of pocket expenses for treatment. This will be achieved by strengthening the existing healthcare service delivery system, targeting the people living in slums and converging with various schemes relating to wider determinants of health like drinking water, sanitation, school education, etc., implemented by the Ministries of Urban Development, Housing and Urban Poverty Alleviation, Human Resource Development and Women and Child Development.

The NUHM would cover all State capitals, district headquarters and cities/towns with a population of more than 50,000. It would primarily focus on slum dwellers and other marginalized groups like rickshaw pullers, street vendors, railway and bus station coolies, homeless people, street children, construction site workers. The center-state funding pattern will be 75:25 for all the States except North-Eastern states including Sikkim and other special category states of Jammu and Kashmir, Himachal Pradesh and Uttarakhand, for whom the center-state funding pattern will be 90:10. The Program Implementation Plans (PIPs) sent by the states are apprised and approved by the Ministry.

The NUHM would endeavor to achieve its goal through:

- Need-based city specific urban healthcare system to meet the diverse healthcare needs of the urban poor and other vulnerable sections.
- Institutional mechanism and management systems to meet the health-related challenges of a rapidly growing urban population.
- Partnership with community and local bodies for a more proactive involvement in planning, implementation, and monitoring of health activities.
- Availability of resources for providing essential primary healthcare to urban poor.
- Partnerships with NGOs, for profit and not for profit health service providers and other stakeholders.

SUMMARY

- Community has well-defined geographical boundaries and is relatively permanent.
- The communication facilities are being extended to rural areas.
- The Central and State Government have several new and old programs, which are useful to bring changes in rural life.
- Although the growth of cities greatly depends on birth and death rates and migration, political, religious, historical and economic factors equally contribute.
- It can be concluded that city or the urban community has a limited area, a local government and some traits, which makes the city entirely different from the rural community.
- The development of community is the basic need of the era that demands a change in the mental outlook of the people, an urge to reach higher standard of life is a strong will to achieve it.
- Panchayati Raj is a three-tier structure of democratic institutions at district, block and village levels, namely, Zila Parishad, Panchayat Samiti and Village Panchayats respectively.
- Janani Suraksha Yojana or JSY aims to reduce maternal mortality among pregnant women by encouraging them to deliver in government health facilities.
- District Hospitals are being strengthened to provide multispecialty healthcare including dialysis care, intensive cardiac care, cancer treatment, mental illness, emergency medical and trauma care, etc.

STUDENT ASSIGNMENT

LONG ANSWER QUESTIONS

1. Define community and explain different types of community and their characteristics.
2. Differentiate between rural community and urban community.
3. Describe community development project.
4. Describe Panchayati Raj system.

SHORT ANSWER QUESTIONS

1. Define the following:
   a. Community
   b. Urban community
   c. Rural community
   d. City
2. How does community engagement contribute to fostering civic participation and social cohesion? Provide examples of community initiatives that promote active citizenship.
3. What are the key challenges faced in building community resilience against social, economic, and environmental disruptions?
4. In what ways do digital communities differ from traditional geographic communities?
5. How has the rise of digital platforms influenced the dynamics of community interactions and collective action?

MULTIPLE CHOICE QUESTIONS

1. **The three-tier system of Panchayati Raj was recommended by:**
   a. Kaka Kalelkar Committee
   b. Simon Commission
   c. Balwant Rai Mehta Committee
   d. Jai Prakash Narain Committee

2. **Unlike village community, urban society lacks in:**
   a. Secondary social control
   b. Social tolerance
   c. Self sufficiency
   d. All of the above

3. **Social distance in a city is due to:**
   a. The size of city
   b. The distance between residences
   c. The social heterogeneity
   d. The traffic problem in city

4. **The spatial feature of urbanization in India has been:**
   a. Localized in nature b. Balanced
   c. Both a and b d. None of these

5. **Which is not a feature of urban life?**
   a. Loss of humanistic value b. Impersonal relationship
   c. Informal ties d. Competition

6. **Who developed the concept of urbanism as a way of life?**
   a. Louis Wirth b. Fisher
   c. Lewis Coser d. None of these

7. **The world's first cities appeared about ....**
   a. 3500 BC b. 300 BC
   c. 2000 BC d. AD 100

8. **Which among the following was an exclusive university town?**
   a. Taxila b. Pataliputra
   c. Nalanda d. Kashi

9. **Which of the following is not one of the features of urban community?**
   a. Face to face relationships b. Complex life
   c. Materialistic d. Glamour in life

ANSWER KEY

1. c **2.** c **3.** c **4.** a **5.** c **6.** a **7.** a **8.** c **9.** a

11

Culture

LEARNING OBJECTIVES

After the completion of the chapter, the readers will be able to:

- Define culture.
- Describe the features and characteristics of culture.
- Understand the nature of culture.
- Define acculturation and assimilation.
- Differentiate between acculturation and assimilation.
- Understand different strategies and outcomes of acculturation.
- Describe the impact of culture on health.
- Define transcultural nursing.
- Discuss the applications of transcultural nursing in nursing process.

CHAPTER OUTLINE

- Culture
- Features and Characteristics of Culture
- Nature of Culture
- Acculturation and Assimilation
- Culture and Socialization
- Transcultural Nursing

KEY TERMS

Acculturation: Assimilation to a different culture, typically the dominant one.
Assimilation: When the original culture is wholly abandoned and the new culture is adopted in its place it is called assimilation.
Culture: Culture is the customs, ideas, beliefs, etc., of a particular society, country, etc.
Transcultural nursing: It is the provision of culturally sensitive and appropriate nursing care to patients from diverse cultural backgrounds.

CULTURE

Culture is the heritage of a society and without culture no society can even exist. It is transmitted from one generation to another. It includes the behavior of an individual in society. India is a country which is very rich in culture and is well known for the culture throughout the world.

DEFINITIONS

- "Culture is everything which is socially shared and learned by the members of a society." **—Horton and Hunt**
- "It is that complex whole including beliefs, art, region, values, norms, ideas, law, taught, knowledge, custom and other capabilities acquired by a man as a member of a society." **—Tylor**
- "Culture is the sum total of integrated learned behavior patterns which are characteristics of the members of a society and which are not the results of biological inheritance." **—E A Hoebel**
- "Culture is the sum total of human achievements, material as well as non-material, capable of transmission, sociologically, i.e., by tradition and communication, vertically as well as horizontally." **—H T Mazumdar**

Culture is the totality of human experience acquired during transmission of heritage from one generation to another and to learn the ways of learning, eating, drinking, behaving, walking, dressing, and working is what describes the culture of an individual.

FEATURES AND CHARACTERISTICS OF CULTURE

Some of the important characteristics of culture have been listed below:

- **Culture is acquired:** Culture is not inherited biologically but it is learnt socially. It is not an inborn attribute but acquired by man from the association of others, e.g., drinking, eating, dressing, walking, behaving, reading are all learnt by man throughout the life.
- **Culture is a social phenomenon:** It is not an individual phenomenon but it is the social process. It develops in the society through social interaction. It is shared by the members of society.
- No man can acquire it without the association of others. It helps to develop the behavior of human beings in a social environment.

- **Culture is shared:** Culture is nothing but the shared belief, values and common behavior that is passed by the people of a territory. For example, customs, traditions, values, beliefs are all shared by man in a social situation.
- **Culture is transmitted:** Culture is transmitted from one generation to the next. Parents pass cultural traits to their children and in return they pass to their children and son. It is not transmitted through genes but through language. Language is the mode of communication which passes cultural traits from one generation to another.
- **Culture is continuous process:** It is a continuous process. It is like a stream which is flowing from one generation to another. "Culture is the history of human race."
- **Culture is accumulative:** Culture is not a matter of month or a year. It is the continuous process of adding new traits and modifying the old cultural traits. Culture is accumulative and combines the suitable traits.
- **Culture is indivisible:** The cultural aspects are inter-related to each other. The cultural development is through integration of its various parts. For example, value system is interlinked with morality, customs, beliefs and religion.
- **Culture is dynamic:** Culture is not static. Cultural process undergoes transformation. But with different speeds from place to place and generation to generation.
- **Cultural diversity:** Every society possesses its own culture and ways of behaving. It is not uniform everywhere but occurs separately in various societies. Every culture is unique in itself and it is specific for a society. For example, values, customs, traditions, religion, belief, practices are not similar but different in every society. However, the ways of eating, drinking, speaking, greeting, dressing, etc., differ from one social situation to another at the same time.
- **Culture is sensitive:** Culture is sensitive to the changing conditions of a physical world. It helps man from all dangers, and natural calamities, e.g., clothes protect us from hot and cold weather.
- **Culture is delightful:** Culture is pleasant and provides all the opportunities for needs and desires satisfaction. These needs may be biological or social but culture is responsible to satisfy it. Basic human needs such as food, shelter, clothing status, fame, money, sex, etc., are all the examples which are fulfilled according to the

cultural pattern. Culture is a process through which human beings satisfy their needs.

- **Culture is related to society:** Culture and society are interrelated like two sides of same coin. Society is a composite of people and they interact each other through it. It is to bind the people within the society.

NATURE OF CULTURE

- Culture is dynamic based on human experiences from time to time.
- A culture is acquired behavior not innate.
- Culture defines attitudes, values and goals of an individual.
- Culture defines myths, legends, and the supernatural powers beyond the explanation of science.
- Culture provides behavior patterns.
- Culture is a continuous process.
- A culture is passed from one generation to other.
- Culture is a qualitative phenomenon.

ACCULTURATION AND ASSIMILATION

Assimilation

When the original culture is wholly abandoned and the new culture is adopted in its place it is called assimilation.

Acculturation

Acculturation is a process of cultural contact and exchange through which a person or group comes to adopt certain values and practices of a culture that is not originally their own, to a greater or lesser extent.

Different Strategies and Outcomes of Acculturation

Acculturation can take different forms with different outcomes, depending on the strategy adopted by the people or groups involved in the exchange of culture. There are five different strategies and outcomes of acculturation (Fig. 11.1).

1. **Assimilation:** It is used when little or no importance is placed on maintaining the original culture and great importance is put on fitting in and developing relationships with the new culture. **Original culture is less important.**

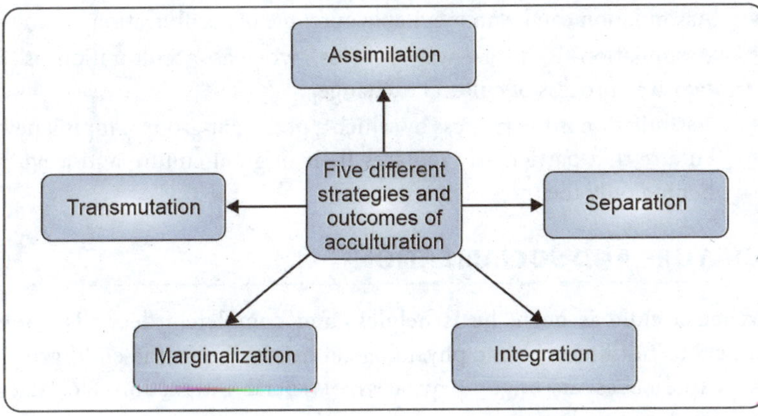

FIGURE 11.1: Five different strategies and outcomes of acculturation

2. **Separation:** This strategy is used when little to no importance is placed on grasping the new culture and high importance is placed on maintaining the original culture. The outcome is that the original culture is maintained while the new culture is rejected.
   New culture is less important.
3. **Integration:** This strategy is used when both maintaining the original culture and adapting to the new one are considered important.
   Both of the cultures are equally important.
4. **Marginalization:** This strategy is used by those who place no importance on either maintaining their original culture or adopting the new one.
   Both of the cultures are not important.
5. **Transmutation:** This strategy is used by those who place importance on both maintaining their original culture and on adopting the new culture, but rather than integrating two different cultures into their daily lives, a third culture is created, which is a blend of the old and the new.
   A third culture is created by mixing two cultures (old and the new).

Differences between Acculturation and Assimilation

Although the two are often used interchangeably, but acculturation and assimilation are two different things.

- Assimilation can be an inevitable outcome of acculturation
- Assimilation is a one-way process, whereas acculturation is a two-way process of cultural exchange.
- Assimilation is the process by which a person or group adopts a new culture that particularly replaces their original culture and leaving behind only the trace elements.

CULTURE AND SOCIALIZATION

When a child is born, he is helpless and completely depends upon others to fulfill most basic physiological needs. But as the child grows he experiences an ongoing process of social interaction facilitates to develop the basic social skills. This ongoing process is called socialization. Socialization is essential for human society because it is the means of teaching culture to each new generation. Therefore, culture is closely related to the process of socialization. Culture includes the pattern of human behavior, values, belief and the materials belonging to a geographical location of society. Since time immemorial culture forms the root of the society.

Common Cultural Practices

- **Use of protective objects:** Protective objects can be worn or carried or hung in the home-charms worn on a string or chain around the neck, wrist, or waist to protect the wearer from the evil eye or evil spirits.
- **Use of substances:** It is believed that certain food substances can be ingested to prevent illness. For example, eating raw garlic or onion to prevent illness or wear them on the body or hang them in the home.
- **Traditional remedies:** The use of folk or traditional medicine is seen among people from all walks of life and cultural ethnic background.
- **Healers:** Within a given community, specific people are known to have the power to heal.
- **Immigration:** Immigrant groups have their own cultural attitudes, ranging beliefs and practices regarding these areas.
- **Gender roles:** In many cultures, the male is dominant figure and often they take decisions related to health practices and treatment. In some other cultures, females are dominant. In some cultures, women are discriminated in providing proper treatment for illness.

- **Beliefs about mental health:** Mental illnesses are caused by a lack of harmony of emotions or by evil spirits. Problems in this life are most likely related to transgressions committed in a past life.
- **Economic factors:** Factors such as unemployment, underemployment, homelessness, lack of health, and poverty prevent people from entering the healthcare system.
- **Time orientation:** It varies in different culture groups.
- **Personal space:** Respect the client's personal space when performing nursing procedures. The nurse should also welcome visiting members of the family and extended family.

Impact of Culture on Health

Health is a cultural concept because health is based on the individual beliefs and the beliefs are directly influenced by the culture therefore culture and health are interrelated. Along with other determinants of health and disease, culture is also one of the important determinants of health.

- The patient's belief about the health and illness affect the adherence to the prescribed treatment.
- Some of the diseases are stigmatized by the society only which is again the common belief of a group of people. For example, most common are psychiatric disorders and sexual disorders.
- The individual may delay seeking healthcare due to social stigma that leads to advanced disease condition at the time of diagnosis.
- The types of health promotion activities are planned according to the beliefs of community and the scope of acceptance.
- The pain perception is affected by culture, in some cultures; tolerance is the norm, even in the face of severe pain. In other cultures, people openly express moderately painful feelings. The degree to which pain should be investigated or treated may differ.
- The place to visit for healthcare is affected by the health belief and culture. Some cultures tend to consult allied healthcare providers first, saving a visit to the doctor for when a problem becomes severe.
- Patient interactions with healthcare providers also vary according to the cultural backgrounds. For example, not making direct eye contact is a sign of respect in many cultures, but a care provider may wonder if the same behavior is their it means patient is depressed.

- The degree of understanding and compliance with treatment options recommended by healthcare providers also vary in different cultures. For example, some patients do not share their cultural beliefs, for not adopting family planning method like use of any contraceptive method.
- The acceptance of preventive or health promotion measures. For example, vaccines, prenatal care, screening tests, etc.
- Perceptions about death, dying and who should be involved in care.
- Certain culture may follow a particular system of medicine such as allopathic or homeopathic, the treatment choice should be made by the patient.

Culture and Role of the Nurse

Illness and wellness are shaped by various factors including perception and coping skills, as well as the social level of the patient. Cultural competence is an important component of nursing. Culture influences all spheres of human life. It defines health, illness, and the search for relief from disease or distress. Religious and cultural knowledge is an important ingredient in healthcare. Healthcare provider needs to be flexible while designing programs, policies, and services to meet the needs and concerns of the culturally diverse population and groups who are likely to be affected by these.

- To develop understanding, respect and appreciation for the individuality and diversity of patient's beliefs, values, spirituality and culture regarding illness, its meaning, cause, treatment, and outcome.
- To encourage developing and maintaining a program of physical, emotional and spiritual self-care, introduce therapies such as Ayurveda and Panchakarma.
- The individualistic approach should be practiced by the nurse.
- Use of direct versus indirect communication. Making or avoiding eye contact can be viewed as rude or polite, depending on culture. Therefore, nurse should be careful about nonverbal communication also.
- To maintain interpersonal relationship with the client, the willingness of the client to discuss symptoms with a healthcare provider and maintaining the privacy of the client's information should always be kept in mind.

- Influence of family dynamics, including traditional gender roles, family responsibilities, and patterns of support among family members are important for the nurse to utilize the available community resources.
- Perceptions about self-image, health, and ageing also affect the health related behavior of client.
- Good communication completes half of the treatment, at the same time poor communication gives a negative image not only for the healthcare provider but for the whole medical community.
- An interaction is adversely affected by cultural bias, and these biases are unconsciously communicated by the healthcare provider, this should be avoided and the professionalism should be practiced.
- Respect, understand and work with different cultural perceptions of effective or appropriate treatment. Ask and record how your patients like to receive healthcare and treatment information.
- When needed, arrange for an appropriate interpreter in case of lingual barrier.
- Listen carefully to your patients and confirm that you have understood their messages.

TRANSCULTURAL NURSING

"Transcultural nursing is a comparative study of cultures to understand the similarities (culture universal) and the difference (culture-specific) across human groups." **—Leininger, 1991**

Application of Transcultural Nursing in Nursing Process

- Determine the client's cultural heritage and language skills.
- Determine if any of his health beliefs relate to the cause of the illness or to the problem.
- Collect information if any home remedy the person is taking to treat the symptoms.
- Nurses should evaluate their attitudes toward ethnic nursing care.
- Self-evaluation helps the nurse to become more comfortable when providing care to patients from diverse backgrounds.
- Understand the influence of culture, race and ethnicity on the development of social emotional relationship, child rearing practices and attitude toward health.

- Collect information about the socioeconomic status of the family and its influence on their health promotion and wellness.
- Identify the religious practices of the family and their influence on health promotion belief in families.
- Understand the general characteristics of the major ethnic groups, but always focus on individualizing care.
- The nursing diagnosis for clients should include potential problems in their interaction with the healthcare system and problems involving the effects of culture.
- The planning and implementation of nursing interventions should be adapted as much as possible to the client's cultural background.
- Evaluation should include the nurse's self-evaluation of attitudes and emotions toward providing nursing care to clients from diverse sociocultural backgrounds.
- Self-evaluation by the nurse is crucial as it increases skills for interaction.

SUMMARY

- Culture is everything which is socially shared and learned by the members of a society.
- Culture is not inherited biologically but it is learnt socially.
- Culture is nothing but the shared belief, values and common behavior that is passed by the people of a territory.
- The cultural development is through integration of its various parts.
- Every society possesses its own culture and ways of behaving.
- Culture is sensitive to the changing conditions of a physical world.
- Culture and society are interrelated like two sides of the same coin.
- When the original culture is wholly abandoned and the new culture is adopted in its place, it is called assimilation.
- Acculturation is a process of cultural contact and exchange through which a person or group comes to adopt certain values and practices of a culture that is not originally their own, to a greater or lesser extent.
- Socialization is essential for human society because it is the means of teaching culture to each new generation.
- Health is a cultural concept because health is based on the individual beliefs.
- Cultural competence is an important component of nursing. Culture influences all spheres of human life.
- The planning and implementation of nursing interventions should be adapted as much as possible to the client's cultural background.

STUDENT ASSIGNMENT

LONG ANSWER QUESTIONS

1. Define culture and explain how culture is related to health of an individual and why is it important for the nurse to understand the culture?
2. What is transcultural nursing and how it is related with nursing?
3. Differentiate between acculturation and assimilation.

SHORT ANSWER QUESTIONS

1. Define the following:
   a. Culture
   b. Acculturation
   c. Assimilation
   d. Transcultural nursing
2. How does cultural diversity contribute to individual and collective identities within societies? Provide examples to illustrate the impact of cultural heritage on shaping personal identity.
3. State the processes of cultural transmission and cultural change. How do these processes influence the evolution of traditions, beliefs, and practices over time?

MULTIPLE CHOICE QUESTIONS

1. **Which of the following best defines culture?**
   a. Biological inheritance passed down from parents to children.
   b. The social process of learning behaviors, beliefs, and values within a society.
   c. The genetic traits that are transmitted through generations.
   d. The innate abilities and talents of an individual.
2. **According to the text, which of the following is NOT a characteristic of culture?**
   a. Culture is inherited biologically.
   b. Culture is a continuous process.
   c. Culture is transmitted from one generation to the next.
   d. Culture is dynamic and changes over time.

3. **What does the term "acculturation" refer to?**
    a. The complete abandonment of one's original culture in favor of a new one.
    b. The process of cultural contact and exchange where a person adopts values and practices from a different culture.
    c. The rejection of any new cultural influences and strict adherence to original cultural practices.
    d. The development of a third culture blending old and new cultural traits.

4. **What role does culture play in health, according to the text?**
    a. Culture has no impact on health beliefs and practices.
    b. Culture only affects mental health perceptions.
    c. Culture influences beliefs about health, illness, treatment adherence, and interactions with healthcare providers.
    d. Culture solely determines dietary habits and exercise routines.

5. **Which strategy of acculturation involves maintaining the original culture while also adopting aspects of a new culture?**
    a. Assimilation b. Separation
    c. Integration d. Marginalization

ANSWER KEY

1. b **2.** a **3.** b **4.** c **5.** c

12

Introduction to Psychology

LEARNING OBJECTIVES

After the completion of the chapter, the readers will be able to:

- Define psychology and describe meaning of psychology.
- Discuss the nature of psychology.
- Understand the scope of psychology.
- Explain the importance of psychology for nurses.

CHAPTER OUTLINE

- Introduction
- Meaning
- Scope of Psychology
- Branches of Psychology
- Importance of Psychology for Nurses

KEY TERMS

Adaptive behavior: It is the age appropriate behavior that a person needs to live independently at home, school and in community.

Affect: It is an act of expressing emotions through the facial expressions.

Belief: It is a state of mind in which something that is accepted is held to be true by an individual or a group.

Emotions: It is a complex feeling that results in physical and psychological changes that result in change in behavior.

Facial expression: Also known as "window to the soul". It is a form of communication used to convey fear, anger, sadness and happiness throughout the world.

Knowledge: A process of understanding someone or something with the help of complex cognitive processes such as reasoning, association, perception and communication.

Perception: It refers to a way sensory information is organized, interpreted and consciously experienced.

Psychology: The scientific study of the mind and behavior.

INTRODUCTION

Psychology is a branch of science which deals with the mental process and behavior. Behavior includes person's verbal and non-verbal expressions, etc. Mental process includes various activities of mind such as memory, thinking, perception, etc.

MEANING

The word psychology is derived from two Greek words, "*Psyche*" means "soul" and "*Logos*" means "study". Hence, psychology is the study of soul. Various psychologists have given the definitions of psychology in their own ways. Some of these definitions are given as follows:

DEFINITIONS

- "Psychology is the scientific study of behavior and mental processes."
  —Pastorino and Portillo
- "Psychology is the scientific study of mental processes and behavior. It is the study of mind and how it works." **—Oxford American Dictionary**
- "Psychology is the scientific study of the human mind and its functions, especially those affecting behavior in a given context."
  —Concise Oxford Dictionary
- "Psychology is the description and explanation of states of consciousness (such as desires, emotions, cognitions, reasoning, decision etc.) in human beings." **—William James**
- "Psychology is a scientific study of conscious experience."
  —Wilhelm Wundt
- "Psychology is the science which aims to give us better understanding and control of the behavior of the organism as a whole."
  —William McDougall

SCOPE OF PSYCHOLOGY

- Psychology has a huge relevance in the nursing practice.
- Nurses have to interact with other professionals to give best quality care to the patients.
- Nurses need to fully understand how other people behave and act in certain situations—and in these instances psychology is a great help.
- While assessing condition of a patient in pain or during treatment, psychology helps a nurse to understand patient's emotions.

- Psychology helps a nurse to know how to interact with patients who come from different backgrounds, and belong to different genders and age.
- Psychology helps to improve the nurse and patient relationship.
- Knowledge of psychology helps a nurse to get the trust of patients. This makes the patients more responsive with the instructions they are given. It further helps the patient to get fast recovery.

BRANCHES OF PSYCHOLOGY

Psychology is a vast field of science and is mainly divided into two main branches.

1. Pure Psychology

Pure psychology provides theories and framework related to psychology. It deals with the formulation of theories, principles and different methods for the assessment of human and animal behavior.

Different Branches of Pure Psychology

- **General psychology:** It deals with the fundamental rules, theories and principles of psychology in order to study human and animal behavior.
- **Abnormal psychology:** It deals with the abnormal behavior of human and animal and its underlying psychopathology. It is also known as psychopathology.
- **Cognitive psychology:** It deals with the higher mental functions of individuals such as thinking, perception, problem solving, memory, learning, language and their way of communication with others.
- **Developmental psychology:** It helps us to explain how a person developed psychologically during his lifetime.
- **Evolutionary psychology:** It studies how the human behavior is influenced by psychological adjustment during the evolution period.
- **Neuropsychology:** It studies the structure and functions of brain in order to understand the behavior and psychological process.
- **Social psychology**: It studies how feeling, thinking and behavior of an individual are affected by the presence of actual or imagined presence of other people.

- **Child psychology:** It deals with the growth, development and behavior of the children.
- **Animal psychology:** It deals with the behavior of animals.
- **Physiological psychology:** It deals with the role of genetic factors, brain, nervous system and neurotransmitters in underlying behavior.

2. Applied Psychology

Applied psychology deals with application of psychological principles, theories and techniques to approach and solve the different practical problems in human and animal behavior and their experiences.

Different Branches of Applied Psychology

- **Forensic psychology:** It is the application of psychology in criminal investigation and law.
- **Clinical psychology:** It tries to bring science, theory and practice related to psychology under one umbrella in order to understand, predict and relieve the maladjustment, disability and discomfort.
- **Occupational psychology:** It studies the behavior of individuals at work. It also helps us to understand the organizational functions such as selection and training of employees, personal relationships, conflict management, etc.
- **Counseling psychology:** Counseling psychology is a specialty that deals with counseling process and outcome, supervision and training. Counseling is one-to-one interaction between counselor and a counselee. It helps to overcome the maladaptive behavior and to solve some of the problems in one's life, which cannot be cured with medications.
- **Health psychology:** It examines how health is affected by behavior biology and social context.
- **Educational psychology:** It is the application of psychological principles, theories and techniques to human behavior in educational situation.
- **Legal psychology:** With the help of psychological principles, theories and techniques, it tries to analyze the behavior of clients, criminals and witnesses, etc.
- **Military psychology:** Application of psychological principles, theories and techniques in the field of military to understand and analyze the behavior.

- **Women psychology:** It deals with psychological factors related to women's development and behavior. It also explains conditions like hormonal influence on behavior changes and mood swing, discrimination against women, etc.

IMPORTANCE OF PSYCHOLOGY FOR NURSES

- Nurses come across variety of patients in their day-to-day life. No two individuals have same nature of psychology. Despite this individual difference, understanding each patient is only possible with the knowledge of psychology. Hence, knowledge regarding psychology is important for nurses to deal with different types of patients.
- Responses of each patient will vary from situation to situation. The responses of a patient during similar situation like a painful episode may be different from one patient to another one. Knowledge of psychology helps nurses to understand the responses of patients in various situations and this can help in coping with the situations.
- Responses to treatment and medical procedure also vary from patient to patient. This variation is due to the individual differences in coping behavior. This behavior can be better understood and explained with the help of psychology.
- Psychological factors of an individual are vital in the development of a disease and recovery from the disease. Therefore, to speed up the effects of ongoing treatment strategies, it is necessary to know the psychology of an individual.
- Knowledge about the psychology helps nurses to explain the relationship between psychological stress and physical symptoms in a patient.
- Understanding differences in attitudes and behavior of patients is necessary for better communication with the patients and their care takers. Here psychology plays a major role.
- Creating a hospital environment, which promotes fast healing and recovery from disease is the duty of whole healthcare team. For creating such environment, knowledge about the patient's psychology is necessary.
- Behavior of diseased person vary from time to time, some may be aggressive and some may be depressed, better knowledge about

psychology helps nurses to act according to the psychological state of the patient. It also helps to support the family of deceased person.

- Knowledge regarding psychology is necessary in different types of treatment modalities such as behavior therapy, play therapy, individual therapy, group therapy, recreational therapy, etc.

SUMMARY

- Nurses need to fully understand how other people behave and act in certain situations—and in these instances, psychology is a great help.
- Knowledge of psychology helps a nurse gain the trust of patients.
- Pure psychology deals with the formulation of theories, principles and different methods for the assessment of human and animal behavior.
- Applied psychology deals with application of psychological principles, theories and techniques to approach and solve different practical problems in human behavior and their experiences.
- Psychological factors of an individual are vital in the development of a disease and recovery from the disease.

STUDENT ASSIGNMENT

LONG ANSWER QUESTIONS

1. Define psychology and explain its scope.
2. Discuss the importance of psychology in nursing profession.

SHORT ANSWER QUESTIONS

1. What are the branches of psychology?
2. What is counseling psychology?

MULTIPLE CHOICE QUESTIONS

1. **The branch of psychology that deals with the analysis of behavior of clients, criminal and witnesses is known as:**
   a. Military psychology
   b. Counseling psychology
   c. Legal psychology
   d. Judicial psychology
2. **The branch of psychology that deals with the individuals' behavior at work is known as:**
   a. Occupational psychology
   b. Organizational psychology
   c. Job psychology
   d. Institutional psychology
3. **All of the following are type of applied psychology, except:**
   a. Occupational psychology
   b. Educational psychology
   c. Forensic psychology
   d. Developmental psychology
4. **The definition "Psychology is a scientific study of conscious experience" is defined by:**
   a. William James b. Wilhelm Wundt
   c. Pastorino and Portillo d. William McDougall

5. **Psychology is defined as the scientific study of:**
   a. People and things
   b. Emotions and beliefs
   c. Perception and religion
   d. Mind and behavior

6. **Most human behavior:**
   a. Can be easily explained
   b. Has multiple causes
   c. Stems from unconscious desires
   d. Depends on social influence

7. **Psychology is a:**
   a. Natural science
   b. Physical science
   c. Biological science
   d. Social science

8. **Psychology as a 'Science of Mind', is defined by:**
   a. Psychoanalysts
   b. Behaviorists
   c. Functionalists
   d. Ancient Greek Philosophers

9. **'Psychology' as the scientific study of activities of organism in relation to its Environment is defined by:**
   a. JB Watson
   b. Sigmund Freud
   c. Woodworth
   d. William James

10. **Abnormal Psychology is mainly the study of:**
    a. Normality of mind
    b. Unconscious level of mind
    c. Subconscious level of mind
    d. Abnormality of mind

ANSWER KEY

1. c **2.** a **3.** d **4.** b **5.** b **6.** b **7.** a **8.** a
9. c **10.** d

13

Structure of the Mind

LEARNING OBJECTIVES

After the completion of the chapter, the readers will be able to:

- Describe Freud's views on structure of mind.
- Explain the concepts of mind.

CHAPTER OUTLINE

- Freud's Model of Mind
- Concepts of Mind

KEY TERMS

Hypnosis: It is a mental state in which patient experiences increased concentration and attention.

Preconscious mind: A state of mind that is concerned about thoughts which a person is not actively thinking but they can be easily recalled when a right trigger is given.

Psychoanalysis: A clinical method used to treat psychopathology within the individuals.

Sigmund Freud: An Austrian neurologist and the founder of psychoanalysis.

Unconscious mind: A state of mind that acts as a reservoir of those emotions, feelings, ideas, memory that are not known to the person.

FREUD'S MODEL OF MIND

The famous Austrian neurologist Sigmund Freud introduced the model of human mind in the essay named "the unconsciousness" in the year 1915.

He divided the human mind into three layers:

1. **Consciousness**
2. **Preconsciousness (subconsciousness)**
3. **Unconsciousness**

He also divided human mind into three components and these are as follows:

1. **Id**
2. **Ego**
3. **Superego**

Freud's View of the Human Mind

As shown in the Figure 13.1, the human mind can be understood by dividing it into three layers, which are discussed as follows:

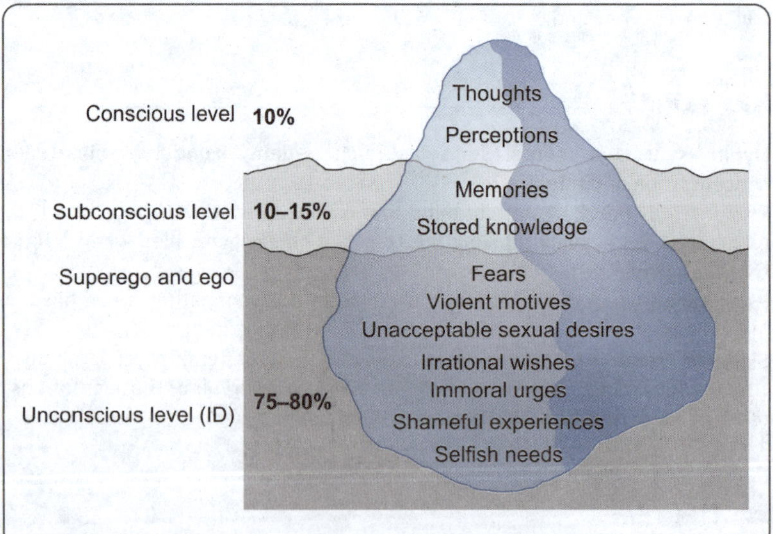

FIGURE 13.1: Freud's view of the human mind: The mental iceberg

Consciousness

This part of the mind deals with the present moment. Because of this component we are aware about something happening in the outside environment and about the activities we are performing. But this part of the mind is only the tip of the iceberg, which we can see above the water level. In reality, the major portion is submerged in the water.

Preconsciousness

This part of the mind is also called subconsciousness. This layer of the mind lies just beneath the conscious layer of mind and it has such kind of information, which can be easily surfaced in conscious mind, whenever and wherever required. Therefore, this layer stores all the information and knowledge gained by an individual through experience or learning. Therefore, this is the memory recall layer of the mind. About 50–60% of information is stored in this layer. When we see the iceberg in Figure 13.1, it may be the layer coming in contact with the surface of water.

Unconsciousness

This layer of the mind indicates submerged portion of iceberg in the water and is the vast portion of the mind. This stores memories and wishes that we cannot access easily. For example, what we are today is because of our past learned experiences since childhood, but majority of these memories are not recallable and accessible. These memories which remain suppressed in the unconscious mind have a tendency to come up in the preconsciousness and conscious mind. Most of our behavior and how we perform in a situation is determined by the unconscious mind rather than conscious mind. During the life process, the memories stored in unconscious mind may move to preconsciousness mind and may even come to conscious mind.

CONCEPTS OF MIND

The id, ego, and superego are a set of three concepts in psychoanalytic theory. They are distinct and interacting agents in the psychic apparatus.

These three concepts are theoretical constructs. They describe the activities and interactions of the mental life of a person.

1. **Id:** Id is present from the time of birth and remains in unconscious part of mind. It is based on the pleasure principle and is most commonly present in a newborn child. Id is selfish, unethical, considers self only and wants to satisfy all the needs and desires. It has no connection with the reality and do not follow any rules or principles.
2. **Ego:** Ego is based on the reality principle and the fact that the person cannot get always what he/she wants. It deals with the rational part of the mind. Ego is the mediator between id and superego. Ego tries to fulfill the need of Id in a reasonable and rational manner. Ego tries to maintain a balance among reality, superego, and id. Ego extends to all the three layers of mind, i.e., to consciousness, preconsciousness and unconsciousness.
3. **Superego:** Superego is the last component of personality to develop and comes into existence around five years of the age. Without taking reality into account, superego strives for more perfections.

Example of concept of mind is well explained in Figure 13.2.

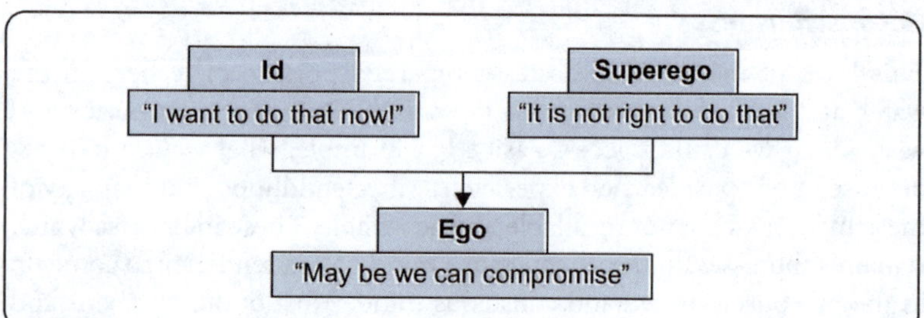

FIGURE 13.2: Concepts of mind

SUMMARY

- The human mind can be understood by dividing into three layers, which are the conscious (for problem solving and logic challenges), subconscious (stores experiences, makes up memory) and unconscious.
- The id, ego, and superego are a set of three concepts in psychoanalytic theory.

STUDENT ASSIGNMENT

LONG ANSWER QUESTION

1. What are the concepts of mind? Discuss in detail.

SHORT ANSWER QUESTIONS

1. Write briefly about unconscious layer of mind.
2. What is ego?
3. Write in brief about id.

MULTIPLE CHOICE QUESTIONS

1. **In Freud's psychoanalytic theory of personality, the pleasure principle is the driving force of the:**
   a. Id b. Ego
   c. Superego d. All of these
2. **................ is the component of personality that deals with the demands of reality.**
   a. Id b. Ego
   c. Superego d. All of these
3. **In Freud's topographic model, the 'çensor' guards the border between:**
   a. The conscious and the preconscious
   b. The conscious and the unconscious
   c. The preconscious and the unconscious
   d. The ego and the id
4. **According to Freud, the odd, magical quality of dreams reflects the influence of:**
   a. Primary process thinking
   b. Secondary process thinking
   c. The 'dream work'
   d. Defense mechanisms

5. **Which of the following statements is true about the ego, according to Freud?**
   a. It exists prior to the id
   b. It follows the 'pleasure principle'
   c. It lends its libidinal energy to the superego
   d. None of the above

6. **Which Freudian defense mechanism does this statement illustrate: 'I'm not jealous, you are'?**
   a. Projection
   b. Repression
   c. Sublimation
   d. Denial

7. **One of these four lists contains concepts from Freud's topographic, structural and genetic models, in that order. Which is it?**
   a. Unconscious, ego, and repression
   b. Unconscious, id, and reaction formation
   c. Preconscious, superego, and regression
   d. Preconscious, superfly, and fixation

8. **Which of the following is not a weakness of psychoanalytic evidence?**
   a. It is subjectivity
   b. It is limited quantity
   c. It is vulnerability to suggestion
   d. It is lack of public availability

9. **Mental state in which patient experiences increased concentration and attention is called:**
   a. Hypernosis
   b. Hyponosis
   c. Stress
   d. Depression

10. **Freud emphasized the role of .... in shaping people's personality.**
    a. Free will
    b. Unconscious desires
    c. Hormones
    d. Group influence

11. **What is the name of Freud model of the mind which is comprised of the id, ego and superego?**
    a. Structural model
    b. Unconscious model
    c. Topographical model
    d. Genetic model

12. **Which layer of human mind stores the information gained by experience or learning?**
    a. Unconsciousness
    b. Preconsciousness
    c. Id
    d. Ego

ANSWER KEY

1. a	**2.** b	**3.** c	**4.** a	**5.** d	**6.** a	**7.** c	**8.** b
9. b	**10.** c	**11.** a	**12.** b				

Notes

14

Psychology of Human Behavior

LEARNING OBJECTIVES

After the completion of the chapter, the readers will be able to:

- Describe the basic human needs.
- Discuss the characteristics of mentally healthy individuals.
- Explain the relationship between body and mind.
- Elaborate the major psychological problems of patients and relatives.

CHAPTER OUTLINE

- Basic Human Needs
- Behavior
- Body-Mind Relationship
- Mental Health
- Emotional Control
- Psychological Problems of Patients and Relatives
- Stress
- Conflict
- Frustration
- Mental Mechanism
- Attitude
- Habits

KEY TERMS

Adjustment: Making small changes to achieve the desired outcome is known as adjustment.
Habit: Any repeated behavior that is learned rather than innate.
Recognition: A cognitive process of remembering coming in contact with a particular person, thing or event that has been previously experienced.
Sensitivity: A state of mind in response to internal and external changes.
Stimulus: Any particular thing that produces an impact on the sensory system of an individual.

BASIC HUMAN NEEDS

Basic human needs are the physical as well as psychological needs of human that help in their growth and development. Abraham Maslow has described these needs as per the hierarchy that are now known as Maslow's hierarchy of needs (Fig. 14.1). Needs, lower down in the hierarchy must be fulfilled before attaining the higher-level needs. From the bottom to top level of the hierarchy, the needs are: physiological, safety, love and belongingness, esteem and self-actualization.

BEHAVIOR

Behavior is the manner in which a person behaves, whether they confirm to the accepted social standards or not.

Factors Affecting Human Behavior

- **Genetics:** Patterns of behavior are influenced by inheritance from parents.
- Early childhood experiences.

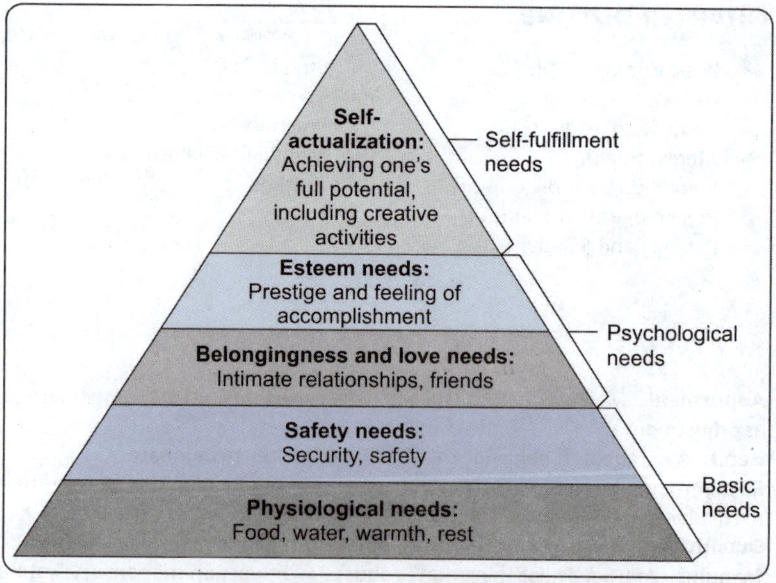

FIGURE 14.1: Maslow's hierarchy of needs

- Social norms shape our behavior and attitudes. Every individual manipulate his/her behavior to best "fit in" with others.
- Core faith and social culture shape our religious faith, philosophical thinking and emotional well-being (e.g., emotions such as shame and guilt connected to moral living).
- **Creativity:** Pushes people past their comfort zone.
- **Attitude:** It is an expression of favor or disfavor, likes and dislikes of a person toward a person, place, thing, or event. The way a person behaves depends a lot on how he looks at the situation.

Types of Behavior

Normal Behavior

- The word 'Normal' is derived from the Latin word 'norma' which means rule. Therefore, 'normal behavior' means that it follows the rule, pattern or standard as set by the society.
- When an individual is able to function adequately and performs daily living activities efficiently and feels satisfied with his lifestyle, he is said to have normal behavior.

Abnormal Behavior

- Abnormal behavior is defined as behavior that is disturbing (socially unacceptable), distressing, maladaptive (or self-defeating), and is often the result of distorted thoughts (cognitions).
- The word 'abnormal' with prefix 'Ab' (away from) means anything away from normal or acceptable.
- It means deviation from the norms or standards or rules.

Dynamics of Behavior

Anything that an individual does such as, act, speak and express is known as behavior. Dynamics of behavior include the factors that are responsible in changing the human behavior. Basically, there are three major factors that change the human behavior:

Physiological

Genetic factors, sex differences, nutrition, illness and inborn disabilities are some of the physiological factors that affect human behavior.

Sociocultural

Social norms, values, family structure, standard of living, impact of modernization, educational status, economical status, social status, etc., are some of the examples of social factors that affect the behavior of an individual.

Traditions, customs, language, cultural norms, values, cultural music, cultural ceremonies are some of the examples of cultural factors that have an effect on the behavior of an individual.

Psychological

Thinking, perception, emotions, attitudes, memory are some of the examples of psychological factors that affect the behavior of an individual.

Motivational Drives

Drive is any urge or force to move in a specific direction and the motive is an arbitrary variable that resides within the individual and intervenes between stimulus and response. Hence, a motivational drive is defined as a state of physiological or psychological arousal that influences how a person behaves. For example, a physiological arousal of hunger or thirst motivates humans to get something to eat or drink. Similarly, a psychological arousal of love, motivates humans to interact with others.

BODY-MIND RELATIONSHIP

Body and mind are interrelated with each other. Both are the two sides of a coin—without one, it is impossible to imagine about the other. Mind grows just as the body grows. Body and mind both are directly or indirectly involved in every activity—whatever we are doing in our daily life. For example, deep thinking and concentration (i.e., mental action) can cause physical fatigue (bodily action). Similarly, rise in blood pressure (bodily action) can cause mental excitement (mental action) (Fig. 14.2).

MENTAL HEALTH

An absence of mental illness is known as mental health. Karl Menninger (1947) defines mental health as, "An adjustment of human beings to the world and to each other with a maximum of effectiveness and happiness".

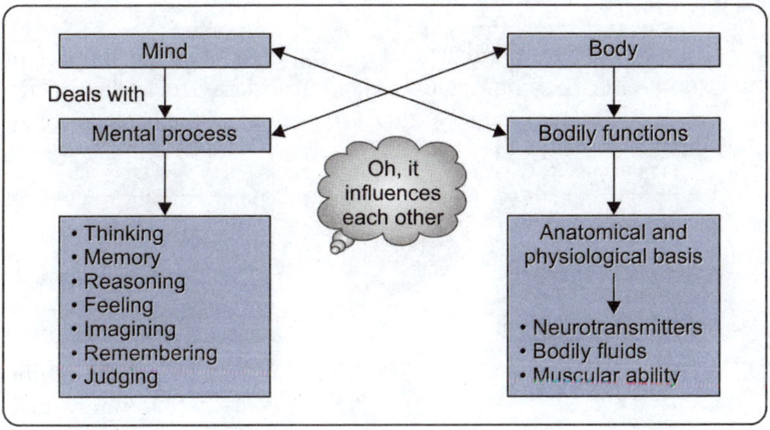

FIGURE 14.2: Body-mind relationship

Characteristics of Mentally Healthy Person

- **Autonomy and independence:**
  - Mentally healthy person is able to make adjustments with other people, situations and surrounding world.
  - He has an ability to solve his problems with his own efforts.
  - He has an ability to make his own decisions.
  - Sense of responsibility is present in mentally healthy person.
- **Accurate perception of reality:**
  - An emotional maturity is shown in his behavior.
  - Tolerance to frustration and disappointments are present in his behavior.
- **Capability for growth and development:**
  - He lives a well-balanced life of work, rest and recreation.
- **Positive view of life:**
  - He has a capacity to give meaning and purpose to his daily activities.
  - He has an ability to understand other's problems.
  - A sense of personal security is present in a mentally healthy person.
- **Environmental mastery:**
  - Mentally healthy person is not affected by the changes in his life to much extent.
  - He takes an obstacle as an opportunity.

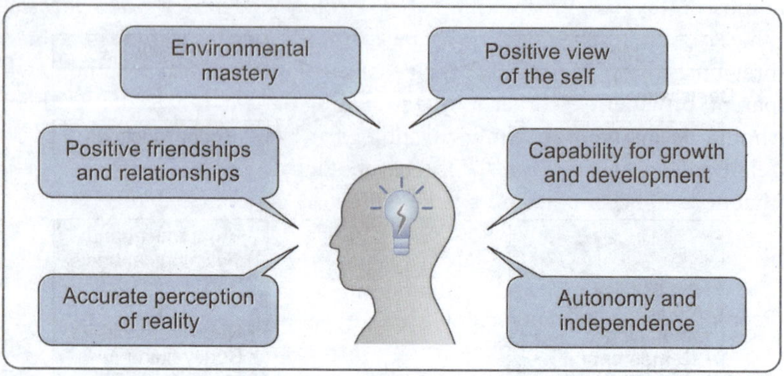

FIGURE 14.3: Characteristics of mentally healthy person

The characteristics of a mentally healthy person are summarized in Figure 14.3.

EMOTIONAL CONTROL

In everyday life, emotions have a powerful effect. Our mood, choices, communication and our relationships all are affected by emotions. Emotions give a color to our lives. Joy, sorrow, fear, anger, sadness, jealousy all are emotions. Emotions can be positive (such as joy, happiness), or negative (anger, sadness). To attain a healthy and peaceful life, balance between both types of emotions is necessary. In order to control over the emotions, following point should be kept in mind:

- Gaining the knowledge about the emotions, their causes and consequences.
- Understanding not only the other's emotions but also one's own emotions, limitations and strengths helps in controlling the emotions.
- Keeping oneself busy by participation in useful activities will direct the attention away from the emotion-provoking experiences.

PSYCHOLOGICAL PROBLEMS OF PATIENTS AND RELATIVES

Illness due to any specific reason leads to psychological problems in the patients as well as his/her care takers. Becoming physically ill is almost always a stressful experience. People who suffer from physical illness often lose an ability to perform a range of activities, which previously have maintained their 'sense of themselves', whether as a parent, provider or worker. While providing patient-centered care, there should be focus on fulfilling psychological needs of patients as well as relatives/care takers. Some of the psychological problems and disorders that need to be kept in mind while delivering patient care are as follows:

Stress

People experience many events that are threatening or that cannot be easily resolved. It leads to stress in life. Stress can lead to physical as well as psychological symptoms in an individual such as anxiety, irritability, impaired concentration, fatigue, disturbed sleep and appetite, etc.

Neurosis

A mild mental illness caused by anxiety, conflicts, ineffective coping and stressful situations. Phobia, obsessive compulsive disorder, post-traumatic stress disorders are some of the neurotic disorders.

Depression

A serious emotional problem characterized by constant feelings of sadness, helplessness, hopelessness, lack of motivation and interest. Sometimes depressed person may take his/her own life due to continuous presence of suicidal ideation.

Mania

A mental disorder characterized by persistent feeling of unusual happiness, talkativeness, confidence, excitement and impulsiveness.

Mild form of manic patients are creative and productive in nature but severe form of mania leads to psychotic symptoms like delusions, hallucinations, etc.

Schizophrenia

A severe mental disorder characterized by delusions, hallucinations, bizarre behavior, disturbed thought, withdrawn from contact with surrounding.

Delirium

A psychological impaired state characterized by confusion, disorientation, apathy, agitation and sometimes illusion. It is also known as "rapid onset of brain syndrome".

Dementia

Any deterioration of intellectual functioning mainly memory, attention and abstract thinking leads to dementia. People who have dementia can forget simple things. Due to this impairment, dementia patients are not able to do simple things. Not being able to keep track of what happens each day. Alzheimer's disease is an example of dementia that usually begins after the age of 55.

Helplessness

Clients in critical care unit demonstrate feelings of helplessness. It relates to feelings of powerlessness associated with being unable to change what is happening.

Hopelessness

In critical care units, patients feel hopelessness that relates to feelings of despondency and loss of optimism. This is reflected in feelings of loss of control (feeling that an event can be managed) and increased dependency on others.

Sleep Patterns and Sleep Quality

Several studies have reported the effects of altered sleep patterns and sleep quality in critical care unit patients. These are bound to have a repercussion on the other psychological parameters.

Low Self-Esteem

Patients in critical care units have feeling of low self-esteem. A person with low self-esteem feels unworthy, incapable, and incompetent.

Body Image Problem

Patients in critical care units have body image problem. It is an idealized image of what one's body should be like that is sometimes misconceived in patients in critical care units.

STRESS

Hans Selye defined stress as, "the nonspecific response of the body to any demand for change". Any situation can be stressful for one person whereas it may be challenging for another. For example, cooking may be a stressor for one who hates to spend time in the kitchen, while it may be an exciting challenge for another who loves to cook.

Nature of Stress

Any reaction to change leads to stress, either in a positive or negative way. Our body and mind both are affected by stress. Under normal circumstances, stress prepares the body for emergency action by stimulating the release of certain hormones like adrenaline, increasing the heart rate, and acceleration of body metabolism. Hence, stress seriously affects person's general health that further leads to decline in daily performance like academic achievements. Therefore, to cope with the stressful events, it is important to recognize the source and effects of stress as early as possible.

Types of Stress

Mainly stress can be of two types:

1. **Acute stress:** Any stressful event that lasts only for a short duration of time comes under this category of stress.
2. **Chronic stress:** Stressful events that extend over time comes under this category of stress. People ignore the chronic stress until they face some abnormal physical symptoms.

Symptoms of Stress

Stress leads to cognitive, physical, emotional and behavioral changes in a person. Some of the symptoms that occurs due to stressful events are as follows:

- Behavioral symptoms—neglecting responsibilities.
- Cognitive decline—impaired memory, concentration and judgment.
- Physical symptoms—increased heartbeat, disturbed sexual function, bodyaches.
- Emotional changes—irritable, unhappy, restless.

Dealing/Coping with Stress

Whenever anyone develops the symptoms of stress, it is prime responsibility to recognize them and take action at once.

Developing a Stress Free Strategy

Using "FARE" approach to deal with stressful events.

- **Flexibility:** Flexibility in your life to accept the changes. Try to find out the solution of problem rather than denying it.
- **Awareness:** To be aware of identifying the source of stress to control the stressful events.
- **Relaxation:** Follow the complete relaxation routine like deep breathing, body massage, physical workout, etc.
- **Exercise:** Routine exercise helps to reduce the stress and maintain the health of body.

CONFLICT

A state of opposition between two or more ideas, interest, goals, etc. When clash occurs between an internal as well as external environment, between two groups, then conflict develops (Fig. 14.4).

Conflict remains as long as an individual is not able to choose one option out of many. Conflict is struggle between people with opposing needs, wishes or demands.

FIGURE 14.4: Conflict

Types of Conflict

According to source, conflict can be of three types:

1. **Interpersonal conflict:** Conflict between parents and children, employer and employee, majority and minor groups, two employees in the same field are some of the examples of interpersonal conflicts.
2. **Intrapersonal conflict:** Conflict within a person such as his desires, goals, and motives are some of the examples of intrapersonal conflicts. Intrapersonal conflicts are also called internal conflicts as these occur within an individual.
3. **Conflict between person and his environment:** Conflicts that occur due to environmental changes such as flood, earthquakes, fire, and war are some of the conflicts that depend on the attitude of the person and he/she has to struggle against these situations.

According to goal, conflict can be of following types:

- **Approach–approach conflict:** When the conflict occurs between two equally attractive goals, then the situation is known as approach–approach conflict. For example, a person may have a desire to watch a cricket match in evening and at the same time, he has to prepare for a class test.
- **Avoidance–avoidance conflict:** When the conflict occurs between two negative goals, then the situation is known as avoidance-avoidance conflict. For example, a student hates to work out his school assignment, but also dislikes the punishment he would receive if he failed to do it. He wants to avoid both the things, if possible.
- **Approach–avoidant conflict:** When the person is attracted to a positive goal but this goal also has some negative characteristics then the situation is known as approach–avoidant conflict. For example, a girl may want to marry, but at the same time, may fear about going away from her home, and her family.

Dealing with Conflict/Conflict Resolution

The process of ending an opposition between two or more desires, motives, goals, persons, etc., is known as conflict resolution. Conflict can be resolved with the help of following methods:

- **Win–lose approach:** Deciding on one solution and leaving behind the other is a win-lose approach.

- **Lose–lose approach:** When neither person is happy with the outcome, then the lose-lose approach occurs. Issues are never resolved under this approach.
- **Win–win approach:** Mutually acceptable outcome occurs in this approach. This is the most effective method of resolving the conflict.

There are some misconceptions or myths about conflicts. Table 14.1 describes some of the myths and truth about conflict.

TABLE 14.1: Myths and truth about conflict

Myth	Truth
Conflict is dysfunctional	Conflict is a normal part of life
All conflicts can be resolved	Most conflicts can at least be managed
Conflicts will go away, if ignored	Conflict can motivate change
Conflicts result in a winner and a loser	Conflict can strengthen relationships

FRUSTRATION

Failure to satisfy a basic need that may be due to any type of obstacle, is known as frustration. Extreme tension leads to frustration. An individual is said to be suffering from frustration when he does not know how to get relief from his tension by himself.

Source of Frustration

Frustration can be caused by many reasons and some of these are:

- Conflict with other people
- Environmental situations that cannot be controlled
- Economic constraint
- Higher level of aspiration
- Social customs, beliefs, traditions, restrictions
- Conflicts within the person

Overcoming Frustration

Frustration can be overcome by keeping in mind the following points:

- Looking at the situation again to know the exact cause
- If required, then modify the goal
- Find out the alternative solution to resolve the frustration

- Accepting the reality
- Think positively
- Withdraw self from frustrated situations
- Increasing one's potential to deal with the situations

MENTAL MECHANISM

Any mechanism used to protect the person from psychological distress is known as mental mechanism/defense mechanism. Mental mechanism helps the individuals to get relief from anxiety associated with frustrations and conflicts. A brief description of various defense mechanisms and their examples are depicted in Table 14.2.

TABLE 14.2: Various defense mechanism and their examples

Defense mechanism	Examples
Compensation: A person makes an attempt to cover up his own weakness by directing his potential on another aspect of life.	An academically weak student may work hard and become the college champion in cricket.
Denial: Refusal to admit an unacceptable idea, behavior or reality.	Person who is critically ill may refuse to admit that there is anything wrong even though he is fully informed about the diagnosis and expected outcome.
Displacement: Discharging one's inner feelings to a less threatening object.	A person comes home after a bad day at work, may yell at his pet dog.
Intellectualization: Using logical explanation to separate the emotions of a painful event.	After being transferred to a new job, that is far away from the home, person hides his anxiety by expanding the advantage of job.
Projection: Blaming another person for own mistakes.	A person who is untruthful may satisfy himself by saying that others too are telling lie and are untruthful.
Rationalization: Justifying one's unacceptable ideas by providing socially approved reason.	A person who cannot do a job well, may satisfy by saying that working hard on this job is not generating good money.

Contd...

Defense mechanism	Examples
Reaction formation: A person behaves in a way that is totally opposite to his real feelings.	A jealous employee who hates his senior may show respect and affection toward him.
Regression: Returning to an earlier and more comfortable level of development.	A person who is not making an adequate progress in learning, may relieve his anxiety by crying or losing his temper.
Repression: Unconsciously forgetting the painful ideas, events or conflicts.	Forgetting the best friend's birthday after a fight.
Sublimation: A person may redirect his unacceptable activities into socially acceptable and desirable activity.	A person having aggressive behavior may transform into competitive sports activity.

ATTITUDE

Observing the things by our own way is an attitude or it is an inherent psychological entity that characterizes an individual on the basis of learned way of thinking.

Kimball Young defined attitude as, "a predisposition to respond in a persistent and characteristic manner in reference to some situation, idea, value, material object or class of objects or person or groups of persons".

Attitude can be positive or negative. A respective attitude toward our elders is a positive attitude, on the other side, a hatred attitude toward a particular person or community is an example of negative attitude.

Developmental Changes in the Attitude

We are born and grown up into a social environment that helps to absorb the attitude spontaneously and passively. In the development of attitude, heredity plays very small role but environmental factors are the major contributors for development of attitude.

Factors Responsible for Change in Attitude

Various factors are responsible for causing developing changes in attitude and these are as follows (Fig. 14.5):

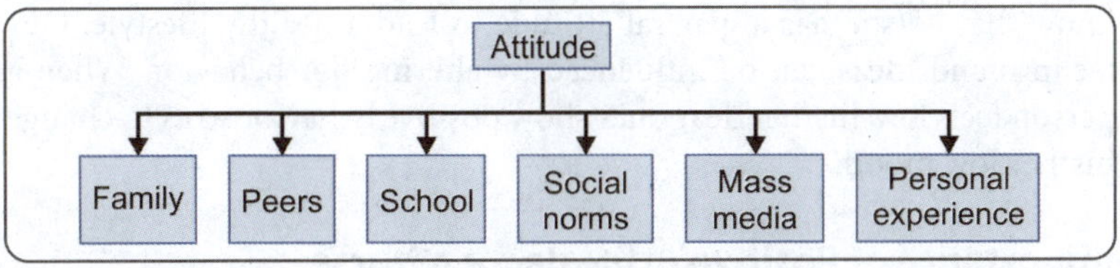

FIGURE 14.5: Factors causing changes in attitude

- **Family:** First interaction with our parents and watching their connection with others helps us in dealing with people. Respectful and courteous attitude of parents is helpful in learning how to respect others without being specifically taught.
- **Peers:** Attitude gets changed through observation also. As the children grow older, they have more opportunities to interact with their peers. Children behave more like their friends. More they interact with their friends, more their behavior changes.
- **School:** School also shapes attitude. Teachers, type of school environment—all lead to major changes in our attitude.
- **Social norms:** Social norms can strengthen or weaken the attitude. Beliefs about what others do, or what others will think if one performs against society norms may impact attitude in a positive or negative way. The social approval and disapproval often guide a person's actions in his/her social settings.
- **Mass media:** Mass media like newspapers, television, movies, radio, etc., are also responsible for shaping our positive and negative attitude.
- **Personal experience:** Personal experience is also responsible for shaping the attitude. For example, if a person had a bitter experience while traveling in roadways bus, then his/her attitude about traveling by roadways bus will become negative.

Effects of Attitude on Behavior

Attitude and behavior are the two sides of coin. If we know the attitude of any person, then by knowing his/her attitude, we can predict the person's behavior. But sometimes people's attitude does not change by changing their behavior. For example, drug addicted persons continue addiction even though they know the dangers of addiction.

Attitude-behavior relationship can be used therapeutically. For example, we may not be able to predict a person's eating behavior if we know that he/she has a general attitude to lead a healthy lifestyle. Our feelings and ideas can be influenced by altering our behavior. When a person feels low, his/her dear ones show positive behavior so as to change his/her low mood.

Importance of Positive Attitude for a Nurse

Nurses have a major role in shaping positive attitude and behavior. By understanding the relationship between behavior and attitude, nurses can analyze the reason of adapting an unhealthy behavior practice.

Positive or negative attitude of person regarding their hospital stay may be the result of his/her own previous experiences. Hence, it is the nurse's responsibility to find out the cause of negative behavior and change this negative behavior into positive behavior that helps in the treatment of patients.

Do you know?

Following traits of attitudes should be kept in mind for becoming a successful and efficient nurse:

- **A: A**mbitious in doing his/her task well
- **B: B**uilding up morale
- **C: C**heerfulness, cooperativeness, making patient comfortable
- **D: D**eveloping a sense of security to patients
- **E: E**fficient and skillful care given to patients
- **F: F**irmness
- **G: G**row professionally
- **I: I**nterest in the problems and difficulties of other people
- **J:** Respect for **j**udgment of others
- **K: K**nowledgeable

HABITS

Meaning of Habit

A particular act that a person does often regularly without knowing that he or she is doing it, is known as a habit.

Formation of Habit

The process by which new behavior becomes automatic is known as habit formation.

Do you know?

3 R's while forming a new habit and breaking bad habit

- **Reminder/Resolve:** Resolution is a strong decisive step that is taken for a purposeful action. Resolution depends on belief in the ability to complete tasks and reach goals.
- **Routine/Rehearse:** Rehearsing the new habit helps in the formation of habit.
- **Reward/Repeat:** A new behavior only becomes a habit once it has been repeated for enough times to make it an automatic behavior.

Breaking of Bad Habits

Bad habits keep away a person from his goals that he wants to achieve in his life. Bad habits not only waste the time and energy of a person, it also alters the physical as well as mental health of a person. Stress and addiction are the major factors responsible for bad habit's formation. Instead of breaking a bad habit, replace a bad habit with a new habit that provides a similar benefit. For example, instead of stopping the bad habit of smoking while you are stressed, you should come up with a different way to deal with stress and picking a new behavior while feeling an urge to smoke.

Importance of Good Habit Formation for the Nurse

Being a nurse is one thing and being a highly efficient nurse is a different thing. A highly efficient nurse should be able to remain calm and focused on his/her tasks in spite of stressful issues. Remaining calm helps in easing the tension. A nurse who has the ability to handle stressful situation calmly has greatest chances of performing the best for the patients.

SUMMARY

- Basic human needs refer to the physical as well as psychological needs of human that help in their growth and development.
- Behavior is the manner in which a person behaves, whether they conform to the accepted social standards or not.
- When an individual can function adequately and performs daily living activities efficiently and feels satisfied with his lifestyle, he is said to have normal behavior.
- Abnormal behavior is defined as behavior that is disturbing (socially unacceptable), distressing, maladaptive (or self-defeating), and is often the result of distorted thoughts (cognitions).
- Dynamics of behavior include the factors that are responsible for changing the human behavior.
- Body and mind both are directly or indirectly involved in every activity—whatever we are doing in our daily life.
- An absence of mental illness is known as mental health.
- Emotions can be positive (such as joy, happiness), or negative (anger, sadness).
- Illness due to any specific reason leads to psychological problems in the patients as well as his/her care takers.
- Hans Selye defined stress as, "the nonspecific response of the body to any demand for change".
- When clash occurs between internal and external environment, between two groups, conflict develops.
- Failure to satisfy a basic need that may be due to any type of obstacle is known as frustration.
- Observing the things by our own way is an attitude or it is an inherent psychological entity.
- Attitude-behavior relationship can be used therapeutically.
- The process by which new behavior becomes automatic is known as habit formation.

STUDENT ASSIGNMENT

LONG ANSWER QUESTIONS

1. What is stress? What is the difference between conflict and stress? Explain.
2. Discuss the psychological problems faced by a patient.

SHORT ANSWER QUESTIONS

1. What is defense mechanism?
2. Write briefly about types of conflicts.
3. What is the importance of positive attitude for a nurse?

MULTIPLE CHOICE QUESTIONS

1. All of the following are types of conflict; except:

a. Intrapersonal
b. Manifest
c. Interpersonal
d. Intragroup

2. Adaptive mechanism of giving excuses when a person cannot solve a problem:

a. Projection
b. Substitution
c. Rationalization
d. Compensation

3. In which defense mechanism anxiety is expressed through physical symptoms?

a. Projection
b. Regression
c. Conversion
d. Hypochondriasis

4. The involuntary blocking of unpleasant feeling and experiences from one's awareness is known as:

a. Displacement
b. Repression
c. Regression
d. Suppression

5. Most commonly using defensive mechanism by a physically abusive individual is:

a. Transference
b. Manipulation
c. Displacement
d. Reaction formation

6. **Imposing one's own weaknesses to others is a defense mechanism, known as:**
   a. Projection
   b. Intellectualization
   c. Suppression
   d. Displacement
7. **Finding a logical reason for the things that one wants to do 'sour grapes' mechanism is:**
   a. Projection
   b. Rationalization
   c. Identification
   d. Sublimation

ANSWER KEY

1. b **2.** c **3.** c **4.** b **5.** c **6.** a **7.** b

15

Learning, Thinking, Reasoning, Observation and Perception

LEARNING OBJECTIVES

After the completion of the chapter, the readers will be able to:

- Define the learning, thinking, reasoning, attention and perception.
- Discuss the nature and types of learning, thinking and reasoning.
- Understand the factors affecting learning, thinking, reasoning, attention and perception.
- Know the importance of creative thinking in nursing.

CHAPTER OUTLINE

- Introduction
- Nature of Learning
- Types of Learning
- Laws of Learning
- Factors Affecting Learning
- Memory
- Forgetting
- Thinking, Reasoning and Problem-Solving
- Creative Thinking
- Observation and Perception

KEY TERMS

Abductive reasoning: It is a form of logical reasoning that starts with an observation and ends after finding the simplest and most likely explanation.

Accommodation: An acceptance of a new information after altering one's existing ideas.

Active learning: An instructional method that engages the students in two aspects: doing meaningful learning activities and thinking about the things they are doing.

Assertiveness: It is an antidote to fear, shyness and passivity and is characterized by behavior of communicating with a calm and positive way, without upsetting others or becoming upset themselves.

Fear: An unpleasant emotional state in response to real and specific stimuli.

INTRODUCTION

Learning is an endless process which starts earlier in the womb of the mother and continues till death. It is one of the most important characteristics of human beings. The experiences during the life time brings about changes in the behavior of an individual and these behavioral changes occur as a result of practice and previous experiences, known as learning.

Any permanent change in the behavior that occurs not because of the maturation but due to the result of practice and experience, is known as learning. Various definitions have been given by different authors and some of these definitions about learning are:

DEFINITIONS

- "Learning is a knowledge acquired through experience or by being taught". **—Oxford dictionary**
- "Learning is a modification of behavior through experiences". **—Gates**
- "Learning is the modification of our readymade behavior due to experiences". **—Colvin**
- "Learning is the process of progressive behavior adoptions". **—Charles E Skinner**

NATURE OF LEARNING

- **Permanent change in the behavior:** Learning is not a temporary change in the behavior but it is a permanent change in one's behavior.
- **Modification of behavior:** Learning is a result of the modification in the behavior that occurs due to the experiences.
- **Purposeful and goal-directed:** Without the proper purpose and direction, no good learning is effective.
- **Active process:** Everyone can learn through his/her own reactions to a particular situation. Hence, learning is an active process.
- **Multifaceted:** Learning is a multifaceted process as it includes various elements such as verbal, perceptual, emotional, conceptual, etc.

For example, salivation of a dog upon hearing the sound of food processed into his dish—the mental process is involved here.

TYPES OF LEARNING

On the basis of degree of complexity, Robert M Gagne gave eight types of learning as per the hierarchy. The lowest four levels of learning focus on behavioral aspects of learning and highest four levels focus on the cognitive aspects of learning. These eight levels are given as follows:

1. **Signal carrying/learning:** It is the simplest form of learning, also known as "classical conditioning". In this type of learning, a condition is given to the learner that helps to produce a desired response—it would not occur naturally. For example, salivation is a conditioned learning that is given to produce a response at the sound of bell (stimulus).
2. **Stimulus-response learning:** This is second level of learning, also known as operant conditioning. This stage is based on the voluntary response of the learner that occurs when the examiner reinforces the learner for his deeper thinking. For example, giving toy to a child when he finishes his homework on time.
3. **Chain learning:** As the name suggests, chain learning occurs when the learner connects two or more previously learned behavior in an order. For example, learning how to ride a bicycle.
4. **Verbal association:** This is the fourth level of learning that occurs when the learner is able to make associations using verbal units. This type of learning is vital in the development of language skills. For example, learning medical terminology and applying it on clinical setting.
5. **Discrimination learning:** This type of learning is focused on the cognitive aspect of learner and is developed when the learner is able to give different responses in similar situations. For example, a patient is suffering with high temperature (fever) after surgery, now it is the responsibility of heath professional to differentiate this high temperature from other types of fever that occurs due to any other reason.
6. **Concept learning:** This type of learning occurs when the learner is able to perform consistent responses to different stimuli. For example, teaching a child about the concept of colors (consistent response) by showing him different colors (different stimuli).
7. **Rule learning:** When the learner learns two or more concepts and apply them in different situations, this type of learning developed.

For example, learning privacy, confidentiality and as per the need, applying them on various situations.

8. **Problem solving learning:** As per the hierarchy, this type of learning is highest in order and is more complex in nature. When the learner is able to solve the problem, this type of learning is developed. For example, as per the need of patients making a nursing process (assessment, diagnosis, planning, implementation, evaluation) in order to solve their problems.

LAWS OF LEARNING

Edward Lee Thorndike (1874–1949), an American psychologist, proposed three major laws of learning and later on he also added few other learning laws. These laws are:

- **The law of readiness:** As per this law, learning takes place when a person is ready to learn. Hence, motivation is important for learning a new thing.
- **The law of exercise:** As per this law, learning takes place only when practicing a particular behavior or act. Hence, for better learning, repetition of any activity is important.
- **The law of effect:** As per this law, learning takes place only when it gives pleasure to an individual. Hence, satisfaction is important for learning.
- **The law of primacy:** As per this law, things that were learned first, create a strong impression on an individual.
- **The law of recency:** As per this law, things that most recently learned are recalled easily.
- **The law of intensity:** As per this law, learning takes place more easily when the learning experience is more dramatic and excited. For example, learning from the real experiences is better than the routine lecture.

FACTORS AFFECTING LEARNING

The success of learning process mainly depends on various factors which are as follows:

- **Nature of learner:** Because of the individual differences, learner related factors play an important role in effective learning and these are:

- **Age of learner:** Learning process is influenced by the age of a learner. For example, a child cannot learn the things that an adult can learn easily.
- **Level of motivation:** Stronger the motivation, greater will be the efforts shown by learner.
- **Intelligency of learner:** Learning takes place as per the IQ level of a person.

  The behavior modifications expected in the learner depends much on the type of learning experience, he receives.

- **Types of learning experience:** Various external factors affect the learning experience and these are:
  - **Working environment:** Light, temperature, noise, etc., are some of the environmental factors that affect learning.
  - **Social support:** Encouragements by the family and teacher also produce positive effects on learning.
- **Characteristics of learning experience:**
  - Learning should be organized well to attain the educational objectives
  - Learning experience should be child oriented:
    - Connect the new learning with the past experiences of learner
    - "Frequent revision and practice" is an order to retain the learned content in mind
    - Learning should be carried out through the utilization of maximum number of senses
    - Learned concepts from different subjects/fields should be correlated to each other
    - Suitable learning methods should be carefully selected for effective learning experiences
- **Resources needed for learning:** Learning is also affected by the availability of resources. The methods required for learning are:
  - Mastery over the subject
  - Good teaching skills of teacher
  - Good teacher-student relationship
  - Length of the working period
  - Teaching-learning aids like charts, overhead projector, blackboard, three-dimensional models, etc.

MEMORY

Learning is an important process in an individual's life and it can be effective only when learned things are used purposefully. In order to use properly, it is important that learned things should be stored in mind and retrieved whenever required. Hence, this capacity of storing and recalling the learning material for future purpose is known as memory.

The word, "memory" is derived from Latin word, "memoria" which means, "mindful or remembering". Thus, remembering information is known as memory.

Various definitions have been given by authors as follows:

DEFINITIONS

- "Memory is the power that we possess to 'store' our experiences and to bring them into the field of consciousness sometime after the experiences have occurred." **—William Ryburn (1956)**
- "Memory is an ability of the organism to store information from earlier learning processes and experiences, retention and reproduction of that information to answer a specific stimuli." **—Eysenk**
- "Memory is the means by which we draw on our past experiences in order to use this information in the present." **—Stromberg (1999)**
- "Memory is a process of maintaining information over time." **—Matlin (2005)**

Types of Memory

Based on the storage of information, memory is categorized into three main types and these are:

1. **Sensory or immediate memory:** Information is stored only for a fraction of second. The sensory memory is further of two subtypes: Iconic and echoic memory.
   i. **Iconic memory:** Storage of visual information for a fraction of second comes under this category.
   ii. **Echoic memory:** For example, storage of auditory stimuli for a fraction of second.

2. **Short-term or working memory:** Storage of information for 15–30 seconds comes under this category. With the help of repetition of same information again and again, this type of memory may be transferred to long-term memory.
3. **Longterm memory:** In this type of memory, storage of information remains for days, months, years and even for a lifetime. This type of memory is again of further two types:
    i. **Episodic memory:** This type of long-term memory is related to the personal information of an individual such as his name, qualifications, date of birth, etc.
    ii. **Semantic memory:** Semantic memory includes things that are of common knowledge. Information related to the ideas and concepts that are not drawn from personal experience comes under this category such as 4 multiply by 4 is equal to 16.

Factors Influencing Memory

- **Age:** Memory change as per the age of the individuals because of the changes in the brain. More is the age of the person, less is he to retain the things.
- **Interest and motivation:** More is the interest and motivation of an individual, better is he able to remember the things.
- **Physical and mental health:** Any abnormality in the physical and mental health of the person leads to impairment of the memory.
- **Methods of memorizing:**
    - **Attention span:** Learning in a place that is free of distraction leads to improvement in the memory.
    - **Practice:** As, "practice makes a man perfect", hence, practicing again and again is important for memorizing the things.
    - **Using abbreviations or mnemonics:** Abbreviations and mnemonics help in memorizing the things easily such as memorizing "IM" to learn the factors affecting memory.
- **Drugs and chemicals:** Drugs and chemicals like alcohol, hypnotic sedatives and certain metals alter the cognitive process and results in memory disturbances.
- **Diet:** A healthy diet which contains antioxidants omega-3 fatty acids, etc., improves the cognitive process in humans. Vitamins like vitamin B_{12}, B_6, Vitamin-E, etc., are necessary for the proper functioning of neurons.

- **Disease conditions:** Medical conditions like brain tumors, high BP, epilepsy, head injury, hypothyroidism, etc., have a negative input on memorization.
- **Sleep or Rest:** Sleep or rest immediately after learning helps for a clear memory by strengthening connections in the brain.

Process of Memory

The memory process is a complex process which involves four factors such as learning, retention, recall and recognition.

1. **Learning:** From every experience, the human brain learns something. The basic unit of memory is engram. An engram is a unit of cognitive information inside the brain. It is said to be the means by which memories are stored as biophysical or biochemical changes in the brain as a response to external stimuli.
2. **Retention:** The engrams are preserved in the brain for future purposes. This process of conservation of memory trans in the CNS is called retention.
3. **Recall:** It is the revival of the past experiences by making use of the memory trans.
4. **Recognition:** It is relationally a simpler psychological process than recall. Recall and recognition are closely related to recognition. The memory trans is stored in a proper rom so that an individual can recollect all the experiences very clearly. But in recall these trans memories are weak or they may disappear. It may result in a weak recollection of previous experiences.

FORGETTING

Forgetting is a failure to recall something, which was learnt previously (Fig. 15.1). In our day to day life, we may forget various things and forgetting things leads to both positive as well as negative impact. For example, it is good to forget the painful experiences in our lives but forgetting to turn off the gas stove leads to negative impact.

FIGURE 15.1: Forgetting

DEFINITIONS

- "Forgetting is failure at any time to recall an experience; when attempted to do so or to perform an action previously learned." **—Drever**
- "Forgetting is failing to retain or to be able to recall what has been acquired." **—Munn**

Types of Forgetting

- **Normal or natural forgetting:** It is the human nature to forget something in a day to day life because it is not possible to retain each and every thing.
- **Morbid/abnormal forgetting:** Forgetting the unpleasant and painful memory, comes under this category.

Forgetting can also be classified as general or specific.

- **General:** When the individual is not able to recall anything that was previously learned, then this type of learning is called general forgetting.
- **Specific:** Individual forgets only a specific part of his earlier learning in this case.

Based on the cause of occurrences, forgetfulness can be classified as

- **Physical forgetting:** Forgetfulness that occurs due to some physical factors such as age, disease, accident, etc.
- **Psychological forgetting:** Loss of memory due to psychological factors such as stress, fear, etc., is known as psychological forgetting.

Factors Affecting Forgetting

- **Age:** Forgetting is directly proportional to increase in age.
- **Time:** As per Ebbinghaus viewpoint, forgetting increases with the passage of time. Ebbinghaus said that after 20 minutes, 72% learned material is retained, after 1 hour 44%, after 6 days 36%, and after 1 month only 21% material is learned.
- **Lack of practice:** Less is the practice, more are the chances of forgetting a thing.
- **Lack of interest and motivation:** Forgetfulness increases due to less interest and motivation from the learner side.

- **Availability of learned material:** Availability and nonavailability of learned material affects the process of forgetfulness.

THINKING, REASONING AND PROBLEM-SOLVING

Thinking, reasoning and problem-solving are considered the chief characteristics of cognitive functions that differentiate human beings from other animals. Because of the presence of these cognitive functions, human beings are more superior than the animals.

Thinking

DEFINITIONS

- "Thinking is a mental activity in its cognitive aspect or mental activity with regard to psychological objects." **—Ross (1951)**
- "Thinking is an implicit problem-solving behavior." **—Mohsin (1967)**
- "Thinking is a behavior, which often implicits and is hidden in which symbols (images, ideas and concepts) are ordinarily employed." **—Garrett (1968)**
- "Thinking is a problem-solving process in which we use ideas/symbols in place of overt activity." **—Glimer (1970)**

Nature of Thinking

- Thinking is a cognitive activity.
- Thinking is a goal-directed activity.
- Thinking is a symbolic activity, which is carried out through signs and symbols or mental images.
- Thinking shifts instantaneously from one aspect to another over a period of time.
- Thinking is a problem-solving behavior.
- Thinking is a process of mental exploration.

Tools of Thinking Elements

- **Images:** These are the mental pictures of an object or a person. These images are based on the previous experiences of a person.
- **Concepts:** Concept is a general idea that represents the common characteristics of all objects in a general group such as when we say "ball" it does not refer to a specific ball but it stands for all types of balls.

- **Symbols and signs:** These are the substitutes for an actual object or experience such as traffic lights.
- **Language:** Language stimulates the thinking process of an individual. An individual gets stimulation to think when he reads, hears or writes words and phrases.
- **Muscle activities:** When we think of a word or we say a word aloud, we use certain muscular responses. These muscular activities have a positive relationship with what we think.
- **Brain functions:** Thinking is basically a function of the brain. The inputs from sensory organs are interpreted and stored in the brain. So, what happens in the thought process is the product of activities of brain.

Types of Thinking

- **Perceptual or concrete thinking:** This is the simplest form of learning that is based on the perception of actual or concrete objects and events.
- **Conceptual or abstract thinking:** This type of thinking is superior than the perceptual thinking. It is an abstract thinking that requires abstract ideas.
- **Reflective thinking:** Thinking, which aims at solving complex problems comes under this category. It is a higher form of thinking as compared to concrete and abstract thinking. This type of learning requires logical arrangements of relevant experiences in response to the solution of a problem. As level of thinking does not require any trial and error efforts, hence, it is an insightful cognitive approach of learning.
- **Creative thinking:** This type of thinking is concerned with the construction of new ideas. Here, the individual himself formulated the problems and tried to resolve it by finding out new relationships and associations in the existing situations.

  For example: Thinking of scientists and inventors.
- **Critical thinking:** It is the most responsible and skillful thinking that leads to a good judgment. It is a higher order well-disciplined thought process. Here the person discovers the truth by stepping aside from his own personal belief system.
- **Nondirected or associative thinking**

  In this type of thinking, the individual thinks without any goal, i.e., he is not having a direction, e.g., day dreaming, fantasy, etc.

Reasoning

To find out the cause and predict an effect, reasoning is the top most form of thinking.

DEFINITIONS

- "Reasoning is a term applied to highly purposeful, controlled and selective thinking." —**Gates (1947)**
- "Reasoning is a process of thinking during which an individual is aware of a problem and identifies it, evaluates and decides upon a solution." —**Munn (1967)**
- "Reasoning is a stepwise thinking with a purpose or goal in mind." —**Garrett (1968)**

Nature of Reasoning

- It is an advanced stage in the process of thinking.
- It is a process with clear cut goals or purposes.
- An individual uses his previous experience or knowledge in reasoning.
- It is a mental search for the reason of an event.
- It involves the problem solving behavior.
- It is a symbolic activity for the solution of a problem and is carried out through symbols, signs or images.
- By following well organized steps through learning, an individual can explore the cause and effect relationship of an event.

Types of Reasoning

- **Inductive resourcing:** This type of reasoning helps to formulate generalized principle by making use of certain facts. For example, a teacher used three dimensional model in the last few anatomy classes, therefore, he will use model in next classes also.
- **Deductive reasoning:** This type of reasoning is exactly opposite of inductive reasoning. Here, an individual starts from an already known generalized principles and apply it in specific case.

  For example: All birds have wings. All wings can help to fly. Therefore, all birds can fly.

Problem Solving

A mental process that involves identifying, analyzing and solving a problem, is known as problem solving.

DEFINITIONS

- "Problem solving behavior occurs in novel or difficult situations in which a solution is not obtainable by the habitual methods of applying concepts and principles derived from past experience in very similar situations."

  —Woodworth and Marquis (1948)

- "Problem solving is any behavior which, through the manipulation of variables, makes the appearance of a solution more probable."

  —B F Skinner (1953)

Steps in Problem Solving Behaviors (Fig. 15.2)

John Bransford and Barry Stain in 1984, enumerated five basic steps in problem solving. These steps are referred to as "IDEAL" thinking.

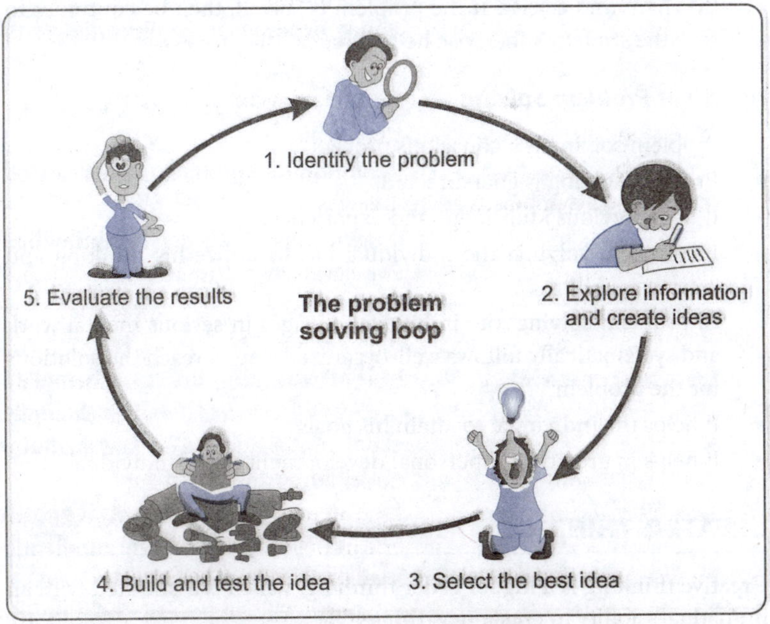

FIGURE 15.2: Problem solving

"IDEAL" Thinking

- **I: Identifying the problem:** Here, an individual becomes aware about the problem that causes difficulty in attainment of goal.
- **DE: Defining and representing the problem:** After the identification of a problem, an individual goes in depth to analyze the extent of problem. It helps him to understand the exact nature of problem so that he can explore the possible strategies for solving it. For the solution of problem, he may collect all the information about a problem, he may read available literature, consult an experienced person, recall his own experiences or think numerous other possible solutions to collect the information.
- **A: Acting on the strategies:** An individual chooses the best possible solution for the problem with the help of all possible solutions. Here, he uses trial and error method to identify the best possible solution.
- **L: Looking back and evaluating the effect of previous activity:** After the use of best possible strategy, an individual analyzes it is positive or negative effect—means whether the problem is solved or still existing. If the problem is still present, he uses another alternative that he found earlier. If the problem is solved, then he continues to save the strategy otherwise he will repeat the process.

Nature of Problem Solving

- Problem solving is a conscious process.
- Problem solving is goal directed.
- It uses previous knowledge and experience.
- In problem solving, the individual has to utilize his thinking and reserving abilities.
- In problem solving, the individual engages in serious mental work and systematically follows well-organized step to reach the solutions for the problem.
- It helps the individual to attain his goals.
- It helps in growth and personal development of the individual.

CREATIVE THINKING

Creative thinking is a higher order thinking, which is associated with an individual's ability to create new things.

It is not bound by any pre-established rules and regulations. It bridges the gap between dream and reality.

Characteristics of Creative Thinking

- It is a universal phenomenon.
- It is an important component of individual's cognitive behavior.
- In creative thinking, the creator is free to think without considering any rules and regulations.
- Although creative thinking is an innate ability, it can be nurtured and nourished by training.
- Creative thinking provides pleasure and satisfaction to the creator.
- The field of creative thinking and its output are vast.

Importance of Creative Thinking in Nursing

Creativity is not a new concept in nursing but creativity among nurses plays a significant role in health and well-being of an individual. Since, nurses provide up to 80% of primary healthcare around the world's health system, it is essential for the nurses to provide creative solutions for correct and future global challenges. Creativity in nursing helps the nurses to shift from traditional task-oriented care to role-oriented care.

Creativity in nursing helps in following ways:

- Brings positive changes in nursing practice
- Improves quality care of patients
- Improves organizational performance
- Gives nurses an opportunity for flexibility, risk taking and support for change
- Improves the communication and cooperation between the nurse and the client
- Improves client's satisfaction regarding nursing care
- Improves client's satisfaction regarding the physical environment of the healthcare institution
- Improves nurse's quality of work, personal and social life
- Leads to development of professional nursing practices and advanced patient care

- Gives nurses a sense of pleasure as they discover something new
- Improves the self-confidence and self-beliefs of nurses
- Leads to innovation, entrepreneurship and is a source of income
- Gives nurses a feeling of empowerment, satisfaction and self-motivation.

Negative Impacts of Creative Thinking

- Consumes lot of time which interrupts family roles.
- Lack of support from subordinates, manager or higher authorities.
- Lack of financial support for creativity.

OBSERVATION AND PERCEPTION

- Perception is seeing a situation from one's own perspective, which is often skewed with different emotions and biases.
- Observation, on the other hand, is being able to see things for what they are, without any hype, emotions or biases.

Attention

Attention is a cognitive function of mind that helps in attainment of a desired outcome. Various definitions have been given for attention as follows.

DEFINITIONS

- "Attention is the concentration of consciousness on one object rather than on another." **—Dumville (1928)**
- "Attention is the process of getting an object or thought clearly before the mind." **—Ross (1951)**
- "Attention can be defined as a process, which compels the individual to select some particular stimulus according to his interest and attitude out of the multiplicity of stimuli present in the environment." **—Sharma RN (1967)**
- "Attention can be defined as the focusing of perception that leads to a greater awareness of a limited number of stimuli." **—Roediger (1987)**

Types of Attention

Ross (1951) classified attention into two types:

1. **Volitional/voluntary attention:** This type of attention is aroused with conscious effort from the individual. Volitional attention exercises the will and demands our conscious effort for arriving at a solution or achieving certain goals. In this type of attention, an individual will have clear cut goals and he/she will remain attentive till the accomplishment of the goal, e.g., answering questions during examination.

   It is again classified into two categories:

   i. **Implicit volitional attention:** This is the volitional attention which is aroused by a single act of will, e.g., the attention paid by the student to complete the work within specified time as he/she is told by the teacher otherwise he/she will be punished.

   ii. **Explicit volitional attention:** This type of attention is aroused by repeated out of will volitional attention, e.g., the attention given during the examination days to score high grades.

   The attention which is aroused without any conscious effort from the part of the individual is called involuntary attention, e.g., attention toward a sudden loud sound.

2. **Nonvolitional attention:** It is further classified into spontaneous and enforced attention.

   i. **Spontaneous nonvolitional attention:** Attention which is the result of properly developed sentiments toward a particular object.

   ii. **Enforced nonvolitional attention**: This is the attention which is aroused by instincts.

   For example: The person who is hungry gives attention to talk or picture related to food.

Factors Affecting Attention

There are certain factors, which affect the attention of an individual's pulse, these are known as the determinants of attention. These are classified as internal and external. These are known as the factors/objective factors.

External Factors

These factors are present in one's environment such as:

- **Nature of the stimulus:** Pictures attract the attention more easily than words. Pictures, which are colorful or contain famous personalities, attract the attention readily.
- **Intensity:** The stimulus with high intensity attracts more attention when compared to a stimulus with less intensity, e.g., bright color gets more attention than dull colors.
- **Size:** Bigger size objects get attraction easily than a small size object. In some circumstances, the reverse also happens, i.e., a small size object in a big background also attracts attention easily, e.g., a small dot in a black board attracts attention easily.
- **Novelty:** New things draw attention easily, e.g., latest fashion dress gets attraction easily than old fashioned clothes.
- **Repetition:** Repeated stimuli get noticed quickly, e.g., teacher repeating a particular point in the class easily attracts student's attention.
- **Movement:** A moving object draws our attention more quickly than a static object, e.g., flickering light easily gets attracted than nonflickering one.
- **Contrast:** An object, which is different from its background draws more attention, e.g., a black dot on a white dress.
- **Change:** A sudden change in the environment draws attention easily.

Internal Factors

Interest, motivation, mood, etc., are some of the internal factors that affect someone's attention.

Perception

- According to Charles Jorris, perception is, "all the processes involved in creating meaningful patterns out of jumbled sensory impressions fall under the general category of perception".
- According to Jalota, "perception is that mental process by which we get knowledge of objective facts".

Laws of Perception

- **Laws of similarity** means grouping the things that are similar in appearances.

- **Laws of closure** means ability to fill the information from past experiences.
- **Laws of proximity** means how the human eye perceives connections between visual elements when seen together.
- **Laws of simplicity** means simple appearance between the objects leads to more enhanced effect of togetherness.

Factors Affecting Perception

- Past experience
- Sense organs
- Motivation and interest
- Physical and mental health

Errors in Perception

Hallucination and illusion are the major errors in perception.

- **Hallucination:** An imaginary perception that occurs without the presence of actual stimuli. For example, seeing the object when it is not present in front of a person.
- **Illusion:** A false perception that occurs even in the presence of stimuli. For example, perceiving the rope as a snake in darkness.

Disorders of Perception

These are divided into:

- **Sensory distortion:** Constant real perceptual object which is perceived in a distorted way.
  - Changes in perception that are the result of:
    - Change in the intensity
    - Quality of the stimulus
    - Spatial form of the perception
    - Distortions of the experience of time
    - Splitting of perception.
- **Sensory deception:** New perception which may or may not occur because of response to external stimuli. These are:
  - **Illusions:** Stimuli from a perceived object are combined with a mental image to produce a false perception. For example, a rope can be perceived as snake.

- **Hallucination:** A perception without an object. It is a false perception, which is not a sensory distortion or a misinterpretation but which occurs at the same time as real perceptions.
- **Intense emotions:** Very depressed patients with delusions of guilt.

SUMMARY

- Any permanent change in the behavior that occurs not because of the maturation but due to the result of practice and experience, is known as learning.
- The lowest four levels of learning focus on behavioral aspects of learning, whereas highest four levels focus on the cognitive aspects of learning.
- Memory is the power that we possess to 'store' our experiences and to bring them into the field of consciousness sometime after the experiences have occurred.
- Information is stored only for a fraction of seconds.
- The memory process is a complex process which involves four factors such as learning, retention, recall and recognition.
- Forgetting is the failure to recall something, which was learnt previously.
- Thinking, reasoning and problem-solving are considered chief characteristics of cognitive functions that differentiate human beings from other animals.
- A mental process that involves identifying, analyzing and solving a problem is known as problem solving.
- Creative thinking is a higher order thinking, which is associated with an individual's ability to create new things.

STUDENT ASSIGNMENT

LONG ANSWER QUESTIONS

1. What is learning? Discuss its types.
2. Explain the factors that affect learning.
3. What is the importance of creative thinking in nursing?
4. What are the types of memory? Describe the factors affecting memory.

SHORT ANSWER QUESTIONS

1. Which factors affect attention?
2. What are the disorders of perception?
3. Write briefly about creative thinking.

MULTIPLE CHOICE QUESTIONS

1. Maturation merely provides a biological pace for:

a. Memory to occur b. Growth to occur
c. Learning to occur d. Thinking to occur
e. None of the above

2. Symbolic concepts become more readily available for use in:

a. Dreams b. Imagination
c. Learning d. Thought

3. Which term refers to the mental activities involved in the acquisition, processing, organization and use of knowledge?

a. Emotion b. Cognition
c. Feeling d. Imagination

4. In which type of memory, the materials are stored for later retrieval?

a. Rote memory
b. Sensory memory
c. Short-term memory (STM)
d. Long-term memory (LTM)

5. **With development, children's memory relies more heavily on:**
   a. Imagination
   b. Symbolic concepts
   c. Gestures
   d. Experiences

6. **Perception is:**
   a. An accurate representation of the world
   b. An appropriate representation of the world
   c. An adequate representation of the world
   d. A native representation of the world

7. **The capacity to learn and adapt to the requirements for survival in one's culture is called:**
   a. Intelligence
   b. Memory
   c. Emotion
   d. Learning

8. **The last stage of creative thinking is:**
   a. Verification
   b. Evaluation
   c. Incubation
   d. Preparation
   e. None of the above

ANSWER KEY

1. b **2.** d **3.** b **4.** d **5.** b **6.** c **7.** a **8.** a

16

Personality

LEARNING OBJECTIVES

After the completion of the chapter, the readers will be able to:

- Define the personality.
- Discuss the approaches of personality.
- Explain the types of personality.
- Describe the various methods about assessment of personality.

CHAPTER OUTLINE

- Introduction
- Meaning
- Approaches of Personality
- Nature of Personality
- Development of Personality
- Types of Personality
- Assessment of Personality
- Importance of Knowledge of Personality for Nurses
- Characteristics of Various Age Groups
- Will and Character

KEY TERMS

Altered consciousness: The term was given by Charles Tart in 1969 and is defined as a state of mind with temporary changes.

Ambivalence: A psychological state of mind when the person is having mixed feelings (positive as well as negative) about a particular subject.

Behavior: An individual response in relation to surrounding.

Cognition: A thought process of acquiring knowledge and understanding about a particular thing.

Mind: An individual's capacity to think, feel and act in response to given stimuli.

INTRODUCTION

Personality is difficult to define, but we know the personality, when we see it. We all make judgment about the personality of people whom we know and even we form the impression about the personality of those people whom we do not know but have only read about.

MEANING

The term personality is derived from the Latin word *persona* meaning the *mask* used by the person when they come in contact with other people. Thus, word personality means the social mask people wear as they assume the roles imposed on them by societal conventions and traditions.

DEFINITIONS

- Personality refers to the quality within the individuals, their behavioral characteristics or both.
- Psychologist, Gordon Allport (1937), defined personality as "the dynamic organization within the individuals of those psychophysical systems that determine their unique adjustment to their environment".
- "Personality is the total quality of the individual's behavior". **—R S Woodworth**
- "Personality is that which permits a prediction of what a person will do in a given situation". **—Cattell**

Hence, from the above definitions, we can say that personality is not a fixed state but dynamic in nature, which changes continuously due to relation with environment.

APPROACHES OF PERSONALITY

- In an integrated manner, personality can be defined as sum total of physical, mental and social qualities of an individual. On the basis of this definition, personality can be studied by two major approaches: psychological and sociological.
  - As per the psychological approach, personality is a style determined by combination of mood swing, emotions and sentiments.

- As per the sociological approach, personality is reflected in terms of person's status and their role in a group.

Approaches to personality are as follows:

Trait approach: The trait approach makes two important assumptions:

1. Personality consists of traits that are unique to each individual.
2. Traits are stable and enduring dispositions.

Psychobiological approach: Focuses on the role of biology in determining personality.

Social learning approach: States that our personality is shaped by what we learn from our experiences.

Psychodynamic approach: Freud's theory proposed that childhood sexuality and unconscious motivations influence personality.

Humanistic approach: The ultimate psychological need that arises after basic physical and psychological needs are met and self-esteem is achieved for the motivation to fulfill one's potential.

NATURE OF PERSONALITY

Various characteristics of personality throw light on its nature and these are as follows:

- **Uniqueness:** Personality is the most important part of what makes us individuals. It is said that no two people look exactly alike; the same can be said about personality; no two personalities are exactly alike.
- **Personality is a dynamic whole:** Definition of personality given by Allport discloses that personality is a dynamic whole. Parts of personality are organized into units that are not static but active.
- **Personality measures the behavior:** Personality of individuals can be assessed by their behavior.
- **Motive force:** There are various motivational theories that help in understanding the dynamics of personality. Person's behavior is overall affected by motives, incentives, ego involvement, etc.
- **Personality is an interaction between heredity and environment:** In a nutshell, personality is the result of the interaction of hereditary characters and environmental factors. Environmental factors affect on the growth and the development of physical, social, emotional and moral characteristics of individuals.

DEVELOPMENT OF PERSONALITY

Personality development is the development of the organized pattern of behaviors and attitudes that make a person a unique individual, and it is recognizable soon after birth. Ongoing interaction of temperament, environment and character helps in the development of personality.

- **Temperament:** Genetically determined traits that determine the child's approach to the world and how the child learns about the world are known as temperament. To specify the personality traits of the person, there are no genes present but some genes do control the development of the nervous system, which in turn controls the behavior of individuals.
- **Environment:** A second component of personality comes from adaptive patterns related to a child's specific environment in the development of individual's personality temperament and environment, both play most important role.
- **Character:** It is the third component of personality, defined as a set of cognitive, emotional and behavioral framework that are learned from the experience of an individual. Although characters depend on inborn traits and early experiences of an individual but it continues to emerge throughout the life of a person.

TYPES OF PERSONALITY

Various psychologists have different personalities classified in various types and these are as follows:

Hippocrates Classification

According to Hippocrates, (a Greek physician known as Father of Medicine), people are grouped into four temperaments:

1. **Sanguine:** Persons belonging to this group are cheerful, vigorous and confidently optimistic.
2. **Melancholic:** Persons belonging to this group are depressed and moron.
3. **Choleric:** Persons belonging to this group are hot tempered.
4. **Phlegmatic:** Persons belonging to this group are slow moving, calm and unexcitable.

Ernst's Classification

According to Ernst Kretschmer (German psychologist), humans are classified into four types. From his study on mental patients Ernst found that certain body types are related with some particular types of mental disorders and these are as follows:

1. **Pyknic:** Individuals belonging to this body type are short, rounded and associated with manic depression. They have the personality traits of extroverts.
2. **Asthenic:** Individuals belonging to this body type have slim body and introverts personality traits. They are more prone to suffer from psychotic disorders such as schizophrenia.
3. **Athletic:** Individuals belonging to this body type have strong body built. They are energetic and aggressive, strong, determined, adventurous and balanced. They are normally associated with manic depressive psychosis.
4. **Dysplastic:** Individuals belonging to this body type have un-proportionate body parts and they do not belong to any of the aforementioned three types (this disproportion is due to hormonal imbalance). Just as the body is unproportionate, their behavior and personalities are also imbalanced. Although this classification of personality is based on the body type has attracted the attention of many psychologists, the theory has been rejected since, it was based on mental patients.

Sheldon's Classification

After being influenced by Kretschmer's view, Sheldon categorized personality on the basis of temperament and body type (Table 16.1). The bodily components are endomorphy, mesomorphy and ectomorphy. The corresponding temperamental dimensions are viscerotonia, somatotonia and cerebrotonia, respectively.

- **Endomorphic (viscerotonia):** This aspect of personality refers to the prominence of visceral organs. Individuals belonging to this group are plump, soft, fat and round-sociable, even tempered and relaxed paunch indicates excess viscera as fat.
- **Mesomorphic (somatotonia):** This aspect of personality refers to the bone and muscle. Mesomorphic has wide shoulders, narrow hips and rippling muscles.

TABLE 16.1: Characteristic features of bodily components according to Sheldon's classification

Sheldon's somatotype	Characters	Shape	Sample pictures
Endomorph (viscerotonic)	Relaxed, sociable, tolerant, comfort loving, peaceful	Plump, buxom, developed visceral structure	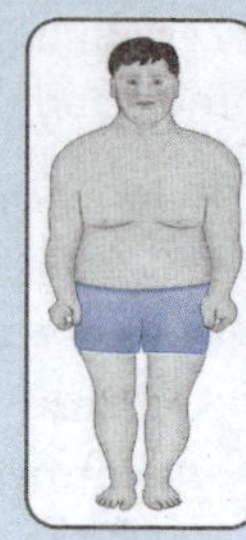
Mesomorph (somatotonic)	Active, assertive, vigorous, combative	Muscular	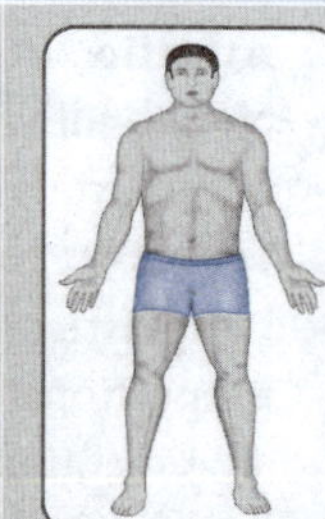
Ectomorph (cerebrotonic)	Quiet, fragile, restrained, nonassertive, sensitive	Lean, delicate, poor muscles	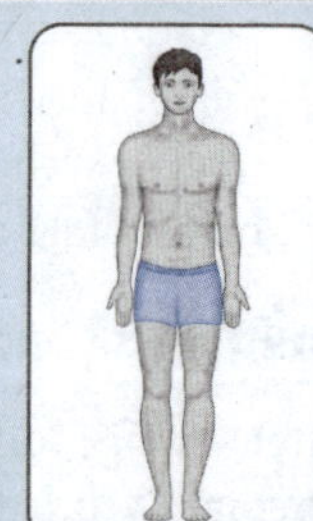

- **Ectomorphic (cerebrotonia):** It is one of the classification given by Sheldon. So, merged it with previous subtypes.

Carl Gustav Jung Classification

C G Jung (a prominent Swiss psychologist was originally a follower of Sigmund Freud) categorized personality into two major groups: introversion, and extroversion and the individuals belong to this group are called introvert and extrovert, respectively.

- **Introverts:**
  - According to Jung, introvert tends to withdraw within himself, especially in times of emotional stress and conflict, characteristics of introverts include shyness and preference for working alone.
  - The introvert likes indoor games and engages in reading and writing books all alone in the corners.
  - They do not like busy peoples/places. Introvert is not that suggestible as other people are. Introvert has some fixed ideas and thinks a great deal before doing anything.
  - Introverts are very sensitive and do not spend much money on others as extroverts do.
- **Extroverts:**
  - The extrovert has some overall opposite behavioral qualities. Individuals belonging to this group are outgoing, extravagant, lively and take a direct action.
  - The extrovert people react positively to different situations and mixes freely with others.
  - They are talkative and expert on making social contact. Extroverts are very generous and outspoken and sometimes more courageous.
  - Extroverts always like outdoor games and do not pay much attention to details. They are always happy, lucky person.
  - Extroverts usually spend a lot of money on others and try to get love and affection from others.
- **Ambiverts:**
  - There are only a few people who are pure introverts or pure extroverts. The remaining majority of people possess both the qualities of introverts and extroverts.

Extroversion—Ambiversion—Introversion

←——————————————→

Preference for *more* stimulating environments	Preference for *less* stimulating environments

ASSESSMENT OF PERSONALITY

According to Dr Saul Rosenzweig, methods of investigating and assessing personality can be divided into the following categories (Fig. 16.1):

- Subjective methods
- Objective methods
- Projective methods
- Psychoanalytical methods

Each one of these categories refers to a number of measuring tools or techniques.

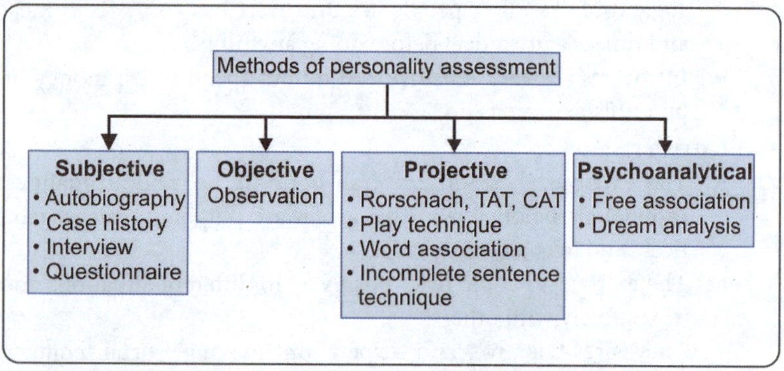

Abbreviations: CAT, children's apperception test; TAT, thematic apperception test

FIGURE 16.1: Methods of personality assessment

Subjective Methods

The subjective methods are those in which the individuals are permitted to disclose what they know about themselves as an object of observation. This method is based on what the subject theirself has to say about their traits, attitudes, personal experiences, aims, needs and interests.

Some of the important subjective methods are as follows:

Autobiography

- The autobiography is a narration by the individual about their experiences throughout the life, their present aims, purposes, interests and attitudes.
- The subject has freedom in selecting experiences that reveal their personality and are significant.

Case History

- The case history is relying to a great or less extent upon the autobiography. In a case history, we combined the information that we obtain from various sources about the individual. This requires many interviews conducted with individual and other persons who know the individual.
- The case study technique provides information about the individual's parents and grandparents, individual's home background, medical history, educational career, friendships, marital life, profession and others.
- This method is helpful in understanding the personality-patterns of an individual who is in a problem or is maladjusted.

Interview

- The interview is the most common method of judging the personality of an individual.
- The interviewer either questions or lets the individual speak freely so as to get a clear picture of the individual. From what individual says, the interviewer knows about their interests, problems, strength and limitations.
- The disadvantage of this method is that it is subjective and is less valid than one believes it to be.

Questionnaires

- Questionnaires are a series of printed or written questions which the person is supposed to answer. Subject is expected to answer each question by checking or encircling or underlining 'yes' or 'no' provided against the question.
- The investigator counts the number of "YES's, NO's" and thus the examiner is in a position to state whether an individual is possessing certain traits or not.
- The limitation of this method is that the individuals may not be willing to disclose correct facts about them or may not be in conscious possession of these facts.
- The method at its best discloses that part of personality which stated clearly or is available to the subject's scrutiny.

Objective Methods

- The objective methods depend on the subject's overt behavior as disclosed to others who serve as observers, examiners or judges.
- Observation about subject is based on certain life situations where their particular traits, habits, needs and other characteristics are brought into play and can thus be observed directly by the examiner.

Projective Methods

- In this method, subject is requested to behave in an imaginative way, i.e., by making up a story, interpreting ink-blots or constructing some objects out of plastic material and drawing what they want to draw.
- Thus, the subject is encouraged to 'project' or throw their thoughts, emotions, wishes and other reactions freely in some situations which are provided. Hence, this method discloses the underlying traits, moods, attitudes and fantasies that determine the behavior of an individual in actual life situations.
- Some of the important projective techniques are—Rorschach test, TAT or thematic apperception test, sentence completion tests, play techniques, word-association method and incomplete sentence technique.

Rorschach Inkblot Test

- Developed by a Swiss psychologist Herman Rorschach (1921), it consists of 10 inkblots having symmetrical designs. Five of these cards are in black and white, two with splashes of red and three in other colors. The test is administrated on individual basis.
- In the first phase, when the card is shown or placed before the client, he/she is asked to tell what he/she sees in the inkblot or what it means to him/her or what this might be.
- In the second phase, called "enquiry phase", examiner finds out not only what the person sees, but also what and how he/she sees it.
- In the third phase, called "testing the limits", the examiner tries to ascertain whether the subject responds to the color, shading and other meaningful aspects of the inkblots or whether the whole or parts of the blots are used by the subject in his/her responses.

- Then the scoring categories of the test such as movement and color are interpreted as signifying different functions of the personality such as intellectual creativity, outgoing emotionality, practical mindedness, etc.

Thematic Apperception Test (TAT)

- TAT developed by Murray and Morgan (1935) consists of a series of 20 pictures. Client is requested to tell the story that each picture suggests him/her.
- These pictures are arranged in appropriate groups for male and female adults and for children.
- On each picture, client tells the story by identifying the characters, explaining their relationships with each other, describing what preceded the situation shown in the picture, and stating an outcome.
- On the basis of major theories such as heroism, sexual interests, vocational ambitions, family conflicts, social status, etc., record of story is analyzed.

Children's Apperception Test (CAT)

- This test was constructed by Bellack in 1948. It is helpful in assessing the personality of children up to 12 years of age by using various pictures of animals or humans in common life situations.
- Before administering the test, psychologist establishes rapport with the children so as to win his/her cooperation. CAT brings to light the child's repressed desires.

Play Technique

- Play technique is more applicable to children than to adults.
- Child is allowed or encouraged to construct the scenes by using dolls, toys, blocks and other building materials.
- Play technique has both diagnostic as well as therapeutic value and is frequently used in child guidance clinics.

Word Association Test

- In this method, client is presented with a list of words, one at a time and with the instruction, client has to respond with the first word that enters in his/her mind.

- The examiner notes the time required for giving each response and the responses themselves.
- Delay from the average amount of time and the content of unusual responses help to identify certain attitudes, anxieties or sentiments of a client.

Incomplete Sentence Technique

- The incomplete sentence technique given by Rotter, Stein and many others is a type of paper-and-pencil personality inventory which has features of an association test as well as of a projective technique.
- The subject is represented with a number of incomplete sentences which he/she finishes in any way that he/she likes.

Psychoanalytic Methods

Psychoanalytic method was given by Sigmund Freud, Father of the School of Psychoanalysis. This test is further subdivided into two main parts:

1. **Free association test:** In this, the person in therapy is told to freely share thoughts, words, and anything else that come to mind. The thoughts need not be coherent.
2. **Dream analysis method:** It is a therapeutic technique best known for its use in psychoanalysis. Freud developed dream analysis as a way to understand the unconscious material of mind.

Both these tests show specificity of the personality, in its unconscious aspect.

- This test requires skilled and experienced psychoanalyst and this is the major disadvantage of this test.

IMPORTANCE OF KNOWLEDGE OF PERSONALITY FOR NURSES

Knowledge of personality formation and change is very essential for nurses.

- With this knowledge, nurse can understand not only about client's personality but also about his/her own personality, which is positive and helping in effective nursing care and, may be negative and affect adversely.

- Hence, nurse should try to understand the personality of patients, and try to change them, if they are negative.
- Relationship with patients may also influence work satisfaction.
- Personality or the way of addressing and presenting yourself to a person you are serving, is of immense importance in the field of work.
- Nurses are the persons, mostly females, who are helping diseased persons, helping them to grow well and healthy again.
- As they have to deal with persons who are both physically and morally down, they should be very cheerful and smiles must prevail on their lips.
- They should have their work satisfaction, and they must do their job with consciousness and concentration.

CHARACTERISTICS OF VARIOUS AGE GROUPS

Erik Erikson's Stages of Psychosocial Development

Unique identity is present in every individual. This identity includes different personality traits that can be positive or negative. These traits can also be innate or acquired, and vary from person to person based on the degree of influence that the environment has on the person.

Erik Erikson's theory of psychosocial development focuses on the sociocultural determinants of development and presents them as eight stages of psychosocial conflicts/development that all individuals must overcome or resolve successfully in order to adjust well to the environment.

According to Erik Erikson's theory, every individual faces a certain crisis in his/her own life that affects their psychosocial growth at each of Erikson's stages of psychosocial development (Table 16.2). Whenever any person experiences such crisis, he/she may be left with no choice but to face the problem and think of the ways that help to resolve it. Failure to overcome such crisis may influence significant impact on their psychosocial development.

TABLE 16.2: Erikson's stages of psychosocial development

Approximate age	Psychosocial crisis	Tasks	Results of unsuccessful task completion
Infant—18 months	Trust versus mistrust	Considering the world as safe and able to be trusted	Doubtfulness, difficulty with personal relationships
18 months—3 years	Autonomy versus shame and doubt	Attaining a sense of control and free decision	Low self-esteem and dependent nature either on people or substances
3–6 years	Initiative versus guilt	Learning new concepts/lessons and practicing these in their real life	Sense of guilt if not fulfill the task
6–12 years	Industry versus inferiority	Self-awareness and confidence increase	Failure leads to sense of inferiority
12–20 years	Identity versus role confusion	Sexual identity develops	Confusion and a feeling of insecurity about whether an activity is age-appropriate for them
20–35 years	Intimacy versus isolation	Attachment with others and loving relationship	Emotional immaturity that leads to feeling of loneliness
35–65 years	Generativity versus stagnation	Contributing something meaningful to the society	Feeling of unproductive member of the society
65 years to death	Ego integrity versus despair	Sense of fulfillment that they have lived their life to the fullest	Failure leads to feeling of hopelessness

WILL AND CHARACTER

Will: It is consciously regulating the activities and behavior by the individuals. "Will" helps in the attainment of set goals by overcoming various obstructions and difficulties.

Will depends on various factors such as:

- Age of individuals
- Physical and mental health
- Amount of training

Character: Strength and originality are an individual's nature that are acquired from education and environment is known as character.

- Character is a lifetime gain of a person. It is the result of growth, it is not innate, which means individuals are not born with character but they acquired it.
- Character may be good and strong like honesty, friendliness, etc., or may be bad such as telling lies, dishonesty, etc.

Normal functioning of will and character leads to a normal personality. On the other hand, any abnormality results in some changes or alterations in personality.

SUMMARY

- Personality means the social mask that people wear as they assume the roles imposed on them by societal conventions and traditions.
- Ongoing interaction of temperament, environment and character helps in the development of personality.
- Sheldon categorized personality on the basis of temperament and body type.
- C G Jung categorized personality into two major groups: Introversion and extroversion and the individuals belonging to these groups are called introvert and extrovert, respectively.
- Personality or the way of addressing and presenting yourself to a person you are serving, is of immense importance in the field of work.
- "Will" helps in the attainment of set goals by overcoming various obstructions and difficulties.
- Strength and originality of an individual's nature that are acquired from education and environment constitute character.

STUDENT ASSIGNMENT

LONG ANSWER QUESTIONS

1. What is personality development? Explain Erikson's psychosocial development of personality.
2. Describe the factors affecting the development of personality.
3. Discuss the classification of personality.
4. What are personality traits? Explain in detail Hippocrates and Carl Jung's classification of personality.
5. Define personality development. Write the classification of any one type (Sheldon classification or Sigmund Freud's classification).

SHORT ANSWER QUESTIONS

1. What are the approaches of personality?
2. What is case history?
3. Write briefly about Rorschach inkblot test.

MULTIPLE CHOICE QUESTIONS

1. Which of the following trait dominates a personality so much that it influences nearly everything a person does?

a. Global trait
b. Cardinal trait
c. Specific trait
d. Central trait
e. Secondary trait

2. Who is the pioneer that proposed the 16 basic dimensions of normal personality and devised a questionnaire (16PF) to measure them?

a. Carl Jung
b. Raymond Cattell
c. Julian Rotter
d. Gordon Allport
e. None of the above

3. **Sheldon proposed three different types of traits. The trait that best describes a football player would be:**
   a. Mesomorph
   b. Endomorph
   c. Ectomorph
   d. Activomorph
   e. None of the above
4. **The idea that you can assess someone's personality by studying their face is called:**
   a. Phrenology
   b. Physiology
   c. Somatology
   d. Physiognomy
5. **The .... complex is to girls as the .... complex is to boys.**
   a. Electra, Oedipus
   b. Oedipus, Electra
   c. Oral, phallic
   d. Phallic, oral
6. **Which of the following is NOT one of the Big Five traits?**
   a. Sense of humor
   b. Openness to experience
   c. Conscientiousness
   d. Extraversion

ANSWER KEY

1. b **2.** b **3.** a **4.** c **5.** a **6.** a

Notes

17

Intelligence

LEARNING OBJECTIVES

After the completion of the chapter, the readers will be able to:

- Understand the meaning and definition of intelligence.
- Discuss the individual differences in intelligence.
- Know the nature and development of intelligence.
- Explain how to assess the intelligence level of individuals.

CHAPTER OUTLINE

- Introduction
- Meaning of Intelligence
- Individual Differences in Intelligence
- Mental Ability
- Nature of Intelligence
- Development of Intelligence
- Types of Intelligence
- Assessment of Intelligence

KEY TERMS

Alfred Binet (1857–1911): A French psychologist, who invented the first practical IQ test, the Binet-Simon test. Hence, known as Father of Intelligence tests/IQ testing.

Chronological age: It is the actual age of an individual.

Emotional intelligence: It was the first introduced by Salovey and Mayer in 1990. It is defined as the ability of an individual to manage one's own emotions as well as to be socially skillfully in nature.

Mental age: It is the mental or perceived age of an individual.

IQ: Intelligence Quotient or mental ratio is the MA/CA, multiply by 100.

INTRODUCTION

In our day-to-day life, we often classify some individuals as bright, some as slow, some can solve problem very easily, some takes long times to handle a situation and so on. All this is possible because of the different levels of intelligence among the individuals.

MEANING OF INTELLIGENCE

The word "intelligence" has been derived from the Latin word "intelligere" that means, "to perceive or understand". As per the Oxford dictionary, meaning of intelligence is, "the ability to acquire and apply knowledge and skills".

Various definitions of intelligence have been given by different psychologist and some of these definitions are as follows:

DEFINITIONS

- "Intelligence is, the ability to adapt to one's surroundings."
  —Jean Piaget (1952)
- "Intelligence is, the aggregate or global capacity of individuals to act purposefully, to think rationally, and to deal effectively with his environment".
  —David Wechsler (1944)
- "Intelligence is, the mental quality consisting of the ability to learn from experience, solve problems and use knowledge to adapt to new situations".
  —David G Myers (2004)

INDIVIDUAL DIFFERENCES IN INTELLIGENCE

Francis Galton (1822–1911) was the first scientist, who studied the individual difference in an organized way. As per his opinion, intelligence level differs from individual to individual. The differences in the intelligence occur due to various factors, some of major factors are:

- Genes are the major factors that are responsible for the variations in intelligence test scores.
- Environmental factors such as living condition, socioeconomic status, training at school, etc., affect the intelligency levels of people.
- Any abnormality in the brain and central nervous system results in low intelligency score.

DEFINITION

"Individual differences are found in all psychological characteristics as—physical mental abilities, knowledge, habit, personality and character traits."

—Woodworth and Marquis

Types of Individual Differences in Intelligence

There are differences in intelligence level among different individuals. We can classify the individuals from supernormal (above 120 IQ) to idiots (from 0 to 50 IQ) on the basis of their intelligence level.

- **Differences due to motor ability:** There are differences in motor ability. These differences are visible at different ages. Some people can perform mechanical tasks easily, while others, even though they are at the same level, feel much difficulty in performing these tasks.
- **Differences due to sex:** Due to sex variation one individual differs from other.
  - Women have greater skill in memory while men have greater skill in motor ability.
  - Handwriting of women is outstanding while men excel in mathematics and logic.
  - Women show greater skill in making sensory distinctions of taste, touch and smell etc., while men show greater reaction and conscious of size-weight illusion.
  - Men are strong in mental power. On the other hand, women on the average, show small superiority over men in memory, language and aesthetic sense.
- **Difference due to age:** Age is another factor which is responsible in bringing individual differences. Learning ability and adjustment capacity naturally grow with age. When a child grows, maturity and development go side by side.

MENTAL ABILITY

Mental ability is the capacity to keep and understand the knowledge. Louis Leon Thurstone was the first who discussed about the mental abilities. Thurstone categorized mental ability into two subtypes: primary and secondary.

Primary Mental Ability

Primary mental abilities could be described as latent core constructs that can explain nearly all cognitive differences. The seven important aspects of primary mental ability (cognitive skills) are:

1. Associative memory
2. Number facility
3. Spatial orientation
4. Perceptual speed
5. Inductive reasoning
6. Verbal comprehension
7. Word fluency

Secondary Mental Ability

- It is a framework, which is made up of cluster of primary abilities and are used for describing someone's intelligence structure.
- Secondary mental abilities are organized clusters of primary mental abilities.

NATURE OF INTELLIGENCE

The nature of intelligence is the ability to learn, adjust and to think well.

Ability to learn: Intelligence is the ability to learn maximum within the minimum time period.

Ability to adjust: Intelligence is the ability to adjust to the surroundings or a new environment.

Ability to think: Intelligence is the ability to think independently and to carry abstract thinking that helps in solving the problems.

Intelligence is the ability to benefits not only from the one's own **experiences**, but also from the experiences of others.

DEVELOPMENT OF INTELLIGENCE

According to psychologists, intelligence continues to increase up to adolescence and declines in old age. The growth of intelligence is at its maximum between 16 and 20 years of age, thereafter the growth of intelligence stops. But, the horizontal growth is acquired. Knowledge and skills may continue to develop till the end of the individual's life, hence, age plays a major role in the development of intelligence.

TYPES OF INTELLIGENCE

Howard Earl Gardner, an American developmental psychologist, known for his theory of "multiple intelligence" put forth a theory where he described types of intelligence. In this theory, he has classified intelligence in seven major categories, but later on, he added a few more classes and some of these are:

- **Verbal-linguistic:** This type of intelligence is concerned with the ability to use words and language. Most common in lecturers, writers, etc.
- **Logical-mathematical:** This intelligence concerned with the ability to think logically and in numerical pattern. Most common in mathematician, philosopher, etc.
- **Visual-spatial:** The ability to visualize the objects comes under this category of intelligence. This ability is most common among navigators, painters, etc.

Theory of Multiple Intelligence

In 1983, Howard Gardner published a book "Frames of Mind". The theory of multiple intelligence, according to this book, has 7 different types of intelligence.

1. **Linguistic intelligence:** This type of intelligence consists of all kinds of linguistic coincidences in individuals. It deals with individuals' ability to understand both spoken and written language and their ability to speak and write themselves. Linguistic intelligence is common among lawyers, lecturers, writers, lyricists, etc.
2. **Logical-mathematical intelligence:** This type of intelligence is concerned with all types of abilities related to logic and mathematics. It is common among mathematicians, physicists and philosophers.
3. **Spatial intelligence:** This type of intelligence is related to spatial configuration and its relationship. It is an area in the theory of multiple intelligence that deals with spatial judgment and the ability to visualize with the mind's eye. The spatial intelligence is visible among engineers, architects, sculptures, navigators, painters, etc., for example, painters manifest this spatial intelligence while they paint on a canvas.

4. **Musical-rhythmic:** An ability to recognize sound and the sensitivity toward rhythms comes under this category. It is most common in musicians, music composers, etc.
5. **Bodily-kinesthetic:** An ability to control one's own body movements and to skillfully handle the objects comes under this category. This is most common in dancers, athletes, etc.
6. **Intrapersonal:** The individual's ability to know about the self, to identify his/her own strengths, feelings, values, beliefs, etc., and to utilize this knowledge in practical situations. It is most common among yogis and saints.
7. **Interpersonal:** The ability of an individual to communicate and to make relationship with others, comes under this type of intelligence.

ASSESSMENT OF INTELLIGENCE

Intelligence varies from individual to individual and exists in a certain amount that again not in the same quantity in every individual. Everything that exists in a certain amount can be measured, hence, to measure the intelligence, various tests are formulated that are known as intelligence test.

Types of Intelligence Tests

On the basis of participants, intelligence tests are classified as:

- **Individual tests:** As the name suggests, individual tests are applied on a single individual basis. As this test involves one to one interaction, hence, serves a diagnostic purpose. To obtain the accurate results it is important to establish a good interaction with the participant, before administering the test. Wechsler scale and Stanford-Binet test are some of the tests that come under this category.
- **Group tests:** As the name suggests, group tests can be applied to the large number of people at the same time. This test was developed at the time of World War I to recruit the people in an army. The army alpha test (AAT) and the army beta test (ABT) were designed.
  - AAT was administered on those individuals who were literate and knew English, while ABT was administered to those individuals who were foreign-born and could not read English.

- Some of other examples of group tests are cognitive abilities test, scholastic assessment tests and multidimensional aptitude battery tests.

On the basis of language and response, intelligence tests are classified as:

- **Verbal tests:** As the name suggests, verbal tests are administered with the help of verbal instructions that should be given as per the language of the participants. The Army Alpha and Stanford-Binet are some of the verbal tests.
- **Nonverbal tests:** Nonverbal tests are not based on the language of the patient. So, these tests do not depend on the literacy of the participants. Raven's progressive matrices and culture fair test are some of the nonverbal tests.
- **Performance tests:** As the name suggests, these tests are based on the performance level of the participants. These tests are totally dependent on the motor responses of participants. Bhatia's Battery of Performance Test, Alexander's Pass Along Test are some of the performance tests.

Advantages

Intelligence tests measure a wide variety of human behaviors better than any other measures.

- They allow professionals to have a uniform way of comparing a person's performance with other people of similar age.
- These tests also provide information on cultural and biological differences among people.
- Intelligence tests are excellent predictors of academic achievements and provide an outline of a person's mental strengths and weaknesses.
- These scores reveal talents in many people, which leads to an improvement in their educational opportunities.
- Teachers, parents, and psychologists are able to devise individual curricula that matches a person's level of development and expectations.

Disadvantages

- Many intelligence tests produce a single intelligence score. This single score is often inadequate in explaining the multidimensional aspects of intelligence.

- Single score can vary greatly in their expression of different talents.
- Knowing the performance on various scales can influence the understanding of a person's abilities and how these abilities are expressed. For example, two people have identical scores on intelligence tests. Although both people have the same test scores, one person may have obtained the score because of strong verbal skills while the other may have obtained the score because of strong skills in perceiving and organizing various tasks.

SUMMARY

- The word "intelligence" has been derived from the Latin word "intelligere" that means, "to perceive or understand".
- The differences in the intelligence occur due to various factors, some of the major factors are—genetic makeup, environmental factors, abnormality in brain.
- Primary mental abilities can be described as latent core constructs that can explain nearly all cognitive differences.
- Secondary mental abilities are organized clusters of primary mental abilities.
- We can classify the individuals from supernormal (above 120 IQ) to idiots (from 0 to 50 IQ) on the basis of their intelligence level.
- Intelligence tests measure a wide variety of human behaviors better than any other measures.
- Intelligence is the ability to learn, adjust and think.
- Knowledge and skills may continue to develop till the end of the individual's life; hence, age plays a major role in the development of intelligence.

STUDENT ASSIGNMENT

LONG ANSWER QUESTION

1. Explain the term intelligence and its types in detail.

SHORT ANSWER QUESTIONS

1. Write briefly about individual differences in intelligence.
2. Write in brief about the development of intelligent behavior.
3. What are the advantages and disadvantages of intelligence tests?

MULTIPLE CHOICE QUESTIONS

1. **David Wechsler defines intelligence as:**
   a. The psychological potential to solve problems
   b. Intelligence tests measure height
   c. Being able to behave in a consistent way
   d. The global capacity to act purposefully, think rationally and deal effectively with the environment
2. **The belief that intelligence is a general ability is a result of the work of:**
   a. Binet
   b. Gardner
   c. Sternberg
   d. Spearman
3. **If it is demonstrated that an intelligence test discriminates against certain ethnic groups, then it can be said that the test:**
   a. Is reliable
   b. Has used a standardization sample
   c. Is valid
   d. Has culture bias

4. **According to Sternberg, intelligence is:**
   a. Made up of three different independent intelligences
   b. A single, general underlying ability.
   c. Made up of eight or more independent mental abilities
   d. A single, specific ability which cannot be measured by traditional intelligence tests

5. **If an intelligence test measures consistently what it is supposed to be measuring each time it is used, then it is said that the test is:**
   a. Based on a normal distribution
   b. Standardized
   c. Valid
   d. Reliable

6. **In terms of intelligence:**
   a. Identical twins are more similar to one another than are fraternal twins
   b. Fraternal twins are more similar to one another than are non-twin siblings
   c. Adopted children are more similar to their biological parents than their adoptive parents
   d. All of the above statements are true

7. **What do the initials IQ stand for?**
   a. Investment in education quotient
   b. Intellect quotient
   c. Intelligence quotient
   d. Intelligence question

8. **The current Stanford-Binet Intelligence Test is descended from the test developed by Binet and Simon:**
   a. In early 1900s
   b. In early 1800s
   c. In early 1600s
   d. In early 1700s

ANSWER KEY

1. d **2.** d **3.** d **4.** a **5.** d **6.** d **7.** c **8.** b

Index

Refer 'f' for figure and 't' for table, respectively.

Section I SOCIOLOGY

E

F

G

H

I

J

K

L

M

N

O

P

R

S

Section II PSYCHOLOGY

O

P

Q

R

S

T

U

V

W

Notes